BRIEN MASTERS is best known amongst children through songs in his *Waldorf Song Book*, and amongst adults through his lectures on 'Music and the Development of Human Consciousness'. His life-long passion for music has led him into a wealth of situations: from prestigious awards (University Barber Scholar 1952) to devoted music therapist for the disabled, from performing before royalty to 'entertaining the troops' on a beer-stained NAAFI piano, from appearing on public platforms (bassoon in Vaughan Williams' *Sir John in Love* in the composer's presence) to the most intimate of occasions (playing in Mozart's viola quintet at a dying colleague's bedside). He has acted as educational consultant up to government ministerial level and has become a widely read author—his Doctoral thesis being in education. Brien Masters is currently Director of the London Waldorf Teacher Training Seminar.

BY THE SAME AUTHOR

MOZART

HIS MUSICAL STYLE AND HIS ROLE IN THE DEVELOPMENT OF HUMAN CONSCIOUSNESS

Brien Masters

TEMPLE LODGE

Published to commemorate Mozart's
250th anniversary: 1756–2006

Temple Lodge Publishing
Hillside House, The Square
Forest Row, RH18 5ES

www.templelodge.com

Published by Temple Lodge 2006

A catalogue record for this book is available from the British Library

ISBN-10: 1 902636 81 3
ISBN-13: 978 1902636 81 8

Cover design by Andrew Morgan
Typeset by DP Photosetting, Neath, West Glamorgan
Printed and bound by Cromwell Press Limited, Trowbridge, Wiltshire

Contents

Acknowledgements

It will be clear to those who read the chapter of this book entitled Credo that my indebtedness for the initial train of thought concerning musical style stems from 'mentors' and friends over many years. That the seeds sown in music itself (my main course of study professionally and otherwise) germinated as they have done here, rather than remaining dormant, is largely thanks to vistas opened up through encounters with A.C. Harwood and Owen Barfield (of the 'Inklings'), Dr Ferdinand Rauter (the first person I met in whom professional musicianship and spiritual-scientific reflections conjoined) and, of course, though only via print, Rudolf Steiner. Any expression of gratitude I could formulate in words to these thinkers would be an understatement. I am grateful to Gottfried Hahn (Stuttgart) whose Class 11 music main-lesson I was fortunate enough to attend. He opened my eyes to the potential benefit that *the development of human consciousness as reflected in music* contained for the layman—he held the rapt attention of a large class of 17-year-olds for a whole week on *The Magic Flute*. Thanks also to my colleagues at Michael Hall in the '70s–'90s who timetabled me many times to give the music main-lesson in Classes 11, compelling me to put my brooding thoughts into appealing (I hope) conceptual form, work that has blossomed across the world in the last 25 years in lectures and workshops on the theme. Technically I am grateful to the early editions of Mozart's works, which I used in preparing the musical examples included in the text and appendices. I would also like to express thanks to the Trustees of the London Waldorf Teacher Training Seminar for appointing Josie Alwyn as Assistant Director during the academic year 2005–06. She took on some of the administrative work of the Seminar which liberated time I needed for writing. Finally, a word of warm acknowledgement to David Lowe who read the draft text and made valuable suggestions. I sought these specifically from a non-professional whose interest lay in similar directions, though in his case more in connection with the visual arts, as I wished the work to be reasonably accessible to the music-loving layman as much as of interest to the informed musician.

Credo

The tourist who does not merely wish to be expensively cattle-trucked by some company through the Grand Canyon together with his digital camera, or whizzed past Stonehenge to the accompaniment of luxury coach music, or trotted round the Louvre by an informed yet uninterested official guide (who can *almost* speak your mother tongue), or urged with others, like a column of ants, through the ancient sanctuaries of Delphi and Olympia ... will almost certainly do his homework before setting out, obtain a guidebook that goes into the kind of detail wherein his interest lies, and ask on-site questions of the courier once the latter's initial *spiel* has opened his mind.

This is a Broad-Church book for the musical tourist, written in the firm belief that specialists of one kind or another, and non-specialists, will hunger for both the highways and byways. The Mozart lover may choose to simply lap up *The Magic Flute*★ or be transported by the *Requiem*★ or wag his toe during *Eine Kleine Nacht Musik*★ without even referring to as much as a programme note—like a thirsty scrambler who cups his hands at a mountain spring and gratefully gulps a refreshing draught, whilst exhilarating in the piquant air of the pine forest and glimpsing far-off peaks that loom and bite into the haze-blue horizon. Fair enough. But there is more behind the sanctuary door than the occasional wisp of escaping incense.

The question is, who is qualified to enter the sanctum sanctorum? Is it the Pharisees who pride themselves on knowing all the rules and who purport to live by them? Or is it those who cherish Mozart in their heart of hearts and who have supplanted the sanctuary and all its trappings with pure evangelical admiration and enthusiasm? Though it is undoubtedly stimulating to exchange findings and views with fellow researchers, I have no desire here to write solely for them, despite the feather-in-cap attraction of seeing one's ideas printed in a refereed journal. Yet nowadays, when even authors of thrillers frequently go out of their way to research certain topics with which they spice their

---

★ Denotes reference in Glossary.

page-turners—French cuisine or highly toxic drugs or the slang of the race track, for instance—and when the hunger for knowledge, pandered to by access to the internet, has resulted in minds obese with information, is the expectation that the reader will be prepared to chew on something in the research chutney he is happily savouring with his curried rice a real problem? No writer can avoid some technical expressions. Music is no exception. We surely expect the architect to speak about walls and arches, sills, chimney breasts, ground drainage or façades. Or the botanist to refer to bulbs and corms, perennials, chlorophyll or grafting. Similarly, if we read about music, we surely expect sooner or later to stumble across mention of sharps and flats, chords, tone-colour, overtures and such like. However, if the architectural text wades into deeper water, such as weepholes, lead flashing or highly technical 'building regs'; or if the botanist strays into more obscure topics such as philotaxis or the Latin name for a rare species of houseleek indigenous to only one of the Canary Islands, we may justifiably expect some help to save us the annoyance of a frequently broken thread of thought while we reach for the dictionary.

But in all this I am far from waving aside specialist knowledge. However, without appearing dilettante, I need to openly declare before it becomes obvious, that I do not presume to write as a Mozart *scholar* in any conventional sense of the word. To begin with, the literature to be read and inwardly digested would require a chunk of a lifetime comparable to that of Mozart's in length! Without being oblivious of scholarship, I am coming from another direction, a direction whose signpost was indicated to me by Sir Anthony Lewis,[1] renowned Handel scholar and Director of the Royal Academy of Music, London. Before his services to music were honoured with a title, I sat at his feet during his lectures on the history of music, which first year undergraduates at the Barber Institute of Fine Arts (where the Music Faculty of the University of Birmingham was housed) were required to attend. Intrigued by his insight into stylistic traits, I took my fermenting mind along to the same course of lectures a second time. Despite all my subsequent postgraduate work being eagerly

---

[1] 1915–1983. In the 'music world' his name is, of course, linked with the publication of *Musica Britannica*.

devoted to music—now over half a century ago—and despite my being selected as Barber Scholar by the University in 1952, music in various shapes and sizes (and here we are mainly focusing on musicology) has been obliged to remain secondary in my career. Conscription press-ganged me into the Royal Artillery and youthful idealism led me into working for seven years with people with special needs, until sober reflection on other urgent problems in contemporary society, combined with more personally motivating life events, finally nudged me towards Waldorf⋆ education as my main professional niche. But secondary does not mean, in my case, marginal or even peripheral. The road to which the Anthony Lewis signpost pointed has led on, winding beside and around the highway of a career in education—in a certain way reminiscent of a caduceus.

At first, there was neither time nor opportunity to do little more than jolly along (rather than substantially increase) the momentum of interest in musical style. Then in the early 1960s I had the good fortune to hear A.C. Harwood give three lectures on the *evolution of human consciousness* as reflected in English literature. Harwood was the closest friend of Owen Barfield. As undergraduates at Oxford they were associated with the Inklings, that small group which included Tolkien and C.S. Lewis.[2] The obituary notice in *The Times* of 13 January 1998 observed: 'Barfield was probably the subtlest and most powerful thinker of the Oxford clique known as the Inklings, and his ideas lie behind the mythic and mystical worlds of Lewis and J.R.R. Tolkien'. The former's connection with Barfield, intimate at a professional level, has been documented in several ways.[3] Unaware of the connection that existed in the prestigious literary hinterland to Harwood's exceptional erudition, I simply came away from those lectures with the feeling, rather nebulous I must admit, that if someone could develop insight into changing human consciousness by diving into literary style, then it must be possible to do the same in music. But it was to be another twice-seven years before my colleagues (Waldorf teachers) asked me to teach a music main-lesson⋆ to Class 11 (17-year-

---

[2] See *Owen Barfield, A Waldorf Tribute*, published by Steiner Education, 1998.

[3] See especially O. Barfield (writing as G.A.L. Burgeon), *This Ever Diverse Pair* (Victor Gollancz, 1950), known affectionately amongst friends as 'The Great War'!

olds), a stroke of destiny which proved climacteric. The mists of nebulous feeling now urgently needed irradiating with clear conceptualization—a long process, which has continued to the present through hundreds of lessons, workshops and lecture-demonstrations given across the world.

The purely musicological road, however, has been lonely—not at all like the highway of education in my life, which has thronged with Waldorf teachers, students, parents, pupils and former pupils as well as journalists, politicians and academics, all of whom have expressed interest in varying degrees in Rudolf Steiner's★ educational ideas. Lonely, that is, from the point of view of specialist colleagues interested in in-depth discussion of the subject itself: until recently, next to no one in the UK; a small, select group of musicians and teachers in Finland with whom I met and worked several times in the late 90s; one or two Israelis; and a handful of music colleagues in South Africa—a music teacher in the northern suburbs of Cape Town and two or three senior academic colleagues at Rhodes University on the occasion of a memorial lecture I gave there for Dr J. Mierowska in 2003. Perhaps the most outstanding fellow enthusiast of all has been Dzintra Viluma who has translated courses of lectures on the theme into three languages: into Russian in Talinn, into Latvian in Riga and into Italian in Bologna. But musicologically lonely is not synonymous with lonesome. These 'happy few' by no means represent the abundance of interest in the subject that is constantly proliferating—and the frequent requests for 'a book'. Hence the present lunge in that direction. And hence my willingness to run the risk of appearing impertinent in raising my head above the parapet alongside what will no doubt be a formidable barrage of Mozart scholarship saluting the celebrations. The Mozart year, therefore, proved to be the *use* of the goad rather than the goad itself.

Finally a word about a Waldorf Class 11. What did Steiner have in mind when recommending aesthetic studies in the arts of painting (and sculpture) for Class 9, literature for Class 10, music for Class 11, and architecture for Class 12? In the present context we do not need to go into the age-relatedness of these subjects for all four classes, though for the pedagogue this is a fertile source of continuous enquiry. All four years offer the opportunity for the Upper School student (ages

14–18 in a Waldorf school) to experience how, *through being reflected in the changing styles in all the arts, human consciousness evolves through the Ages.* There are sound pedagogical reasons, too, for studying this with adolescents, predominantly through the arts and not, say, via science or via the minutiae of daily life, such as those shards from the close examination of which the archaeologist makes his deductions. So, concentrating here on music, it is, it seems to me, significant that this particular study comes at age 17, at the point in adolescence when the search for self-identity—and as often as not for some direction for the immediate future—emerges from the emotional turmoil and confusion that usually accompanies the odyssey that the individuality has to undergo as it voyages through the buffetings and doldrums, the dark storms and false dawns of puberty.

I shall fully return to this theme in the section entitled *Johann*, though not merely from the necessarily restricted aspect of school pedagogy, of course. In fact, the one thing that performer and listener, professional and amateur, musicological researcher and practical musician have in common is the *self.* With this in mind, the book could be taken as an attempt as much to describe the self's journey towards the richness of Mozart's musical style as it is to shed Mozartean light onto the self as the central element in the human constitution. The former perspective is a comment on the significance of his genius appearing in the second half of the eighteenth century. The latter has relevance, among other things, for the debate on and understanding of the so-called Mozart effect today, whether we try to deepen our technical knowledge of what the more recognized researchers are looking at or whether, in more general terms, we confine our interest to the overall effect of listening to Mozart. 'Confine' is hardly an adequate concept. However, this is to anticipate the thoughts that follow.

Brien Masters
27 January 2006

AMADEUS

[These are personalities who] more or less set the tone of an age. In the case of such persons, the biography is of much less importance than what is revealed by their place in the entire process of developing humanity.

Rudolf Steiner, 3 September 1916

The aim of this practical new edition has been the creation of an authentic note-text, clearly indicating Mozart's style . . . [my emphasis].

C.A. Matienssen and Wilhelm Weismann[1]

---

[1] From the Preface of *W.A. Mozart Sonaten für Klavier zu zwei Händen* (no date) edited by C.A. Matienssen and Wilhelm Weismann, C.F. Peters. Here *style* is seen as the way to play the music so that as far as possible it sounds as it did in Mozart's day, i.e. as Mozart intended it.

Praeludium

The year 2006 being the 250th anniversary of Mozart's birth,[1] to celebrate his genius in as many ways as possible needs no excuse. Even so, yet another book *about* him might not seem justifiably celebratory—unless it brings some new perspective to layman and professional alike, which I hope the present work will be perceived to have done, though in offering it I naturally revisit themes that are familiar from the past.

Many of my friends who saw the play *Amadeus*[2] assured me that while brilliantly stage-crafted and entertaining in its own way, that way led more to the ephemeral Mozart than the eternal. This need not be unduly surprising, however disappointing for some. Our public library shelves are sagging with biographies that bulge with trivia. On the one hand, a birth anniversary can be argued to coax our attention back to the ephemeral—ephemeral in the sense of temporal: that which was connected with the person's so-called arrival on earth, their subsequent life span and the path of personal development it encompassed. On the other hand, looking at the significance of an earthly life a quarter of a millennium on would strongly suggest that there is something in it of value far beyond what is represented by externalities, such as speculating on the hatred of jealous rivals and the extent to which that hatred might lead them, or focusing on such details as the hand that dipped the quill into the ink well and squiggled brigades of inky shapes onto manuscript paper, thereby leaving posterity a stack of musical scores.

Anyone who has been at a performance of, say, the 'Jupiter' Symphony★ and experienced the audience explode into a roar of applause as thunderous as that produced by the volcanic blaze of brass at the final apotheosis of a Bruckner★ symphony will need no persuading that a rare spirit was deeply involved in what has just been performed. The abiding popularity of his operas, the curious spotlight

[1] 27 January 1756–5 December 1791.
[2] Peter Shaffer, 1984.

recently directed towards the so-called 'Mozart effect', the uncrum-
bling plinth upon which the zealot places the lofty reputation of his
string quartets,★ these and kindred phenomena all attest to his effervescent yet enigmatic genius. Those critics who have stood out from
the ranks of commentators in the past and judged Mozart by his
contemporary success—the number of his works published before his
'untimely' death etc.—may easily fall prey to the conclusion: here was
genius born before its time. Pauper's-grave thinking of that ilk cannot
be compared with what we are seeking here, any more than glaucoma
can be compared with insight. Mozart's musical inheritance combined
with his genius, to endow us with masterpieces in which his *style* could
only have blossomed in the climate of the precise age in which he
lived. That only comparatively few of his contemporaries recognized
this (Haydn★ and Goethe★ foremost amongst them, and what greater
testimonials could one wish for?) and thus began gathering the
Mozartean fruits of the harvest, gives no real indication of how that
harvest has nourished the rest of us, or indeed, must have nourished to
some extent those who heard many of his world premières but who
either did not develop, or even resisted developing, the 'ears to hear'
what they were listening to.

A major concern of any writer on a specialist subject—or one that
could reasonably be presumed to be specialist: *the style of Mozart and its
place in the evolution of human consciousness* for example—is that only
those with the requisite specialist knowledge are equipped sufficiently
to follow the train of thought. So here, with the help of footnotes, a
glossary and appendices, I have attempted to keep the narrative
flowing along its main course but with invitations *en route* to enjoy a
few technical detours. In the case of Mozart, his genius not only offers
the ear of the passive patron—if that is not an unfair description—
unfading pleasure: at the same time it presents the one wishing to be
more actively involved in the composer's supreme and complex art
with profound riddles. Working towards solving those riddles, I
believe, can increase the pleasure of the listener as well as shed light on
the marvel of the human mind, and indeed even assist the flow of
spiritual energy to descend from that mysterious source, whatever it
was, to which Mozart clearly had access, and of which the rest of us

have clearly become impoverished, if not destitute. Thus my present aims, extrapolated rather than distilled from the above somewhat aphoristic paragraphs, are fourfold:

- to join worthily the swelling chorus which has paid tribute to Mozart's genius;
- to enable the listener to derive greater pleasure from his music and possibly thereby come closer to the meaning of life;
- to add some knowledge to, and thus hope to engender, further research into the art of music itself, in its widest possible spectrum;
- to assist the thrust of awakening spirituality in present day culture, hell-bent, as it otherwise often seems, on blindly stampeding in so many ways towards the ample jaws of materialism.

Analysing and appraising can, of course, easily crush the miracle of the butterfly's wings. I trust I shall not be judged guilty of that in what follows, despite the detail that such an enquiry is going to necessitate.

In addition to the above—though it would be too presumptuous to call it an aim—is the hope that, through digging for certain gold nuggets in the work of Mozart, I lend encouragement to future biographers to discover the vein of the eternal. In his postlude to Thomas Meyer's biography of D.N. Dunlop (inaugurator of the World Energy Conferences in 1924)[3] Owen Barfield expressed his conviction that Meyer had opened the door to a new style of bio-graphical genre. This is certainly worth noting. Without rambling into Romantic diffusion, a bit more of the Psalmist's 'I will lift up mine eyes unto the hills, from whence cometh my strength' would not do us any harm, rather than plunging our biographical microscopes into endless labyrinths of scatological sewers and trawling our enquiry through ultra-personal trivia, where floweth the effluent of our all-too-fallible and frequently misspent strength!

Finally, an odd thing that occurred to me while writing the book was the intriguing phenomenon of Mozart's Christian names. *The New Grove: Dictionary of Music and Musicians*[4] lists four: Johann Chrysostom Wolfgang Amadeus, and I have no reason to quarrel with

---

[3] See T.H. Meyer, *D.N. Dunlop: A Biography* (translated by Ian Bass, Temple Lodge Publishing, 1982). The first occasion bore the title 'World Power Con-ference'.

[4] 1980, Macmillan, Stanley Sadie (ed.).

the dictionary's superiority in such respects. But my memory is woven through with having seen here and there references to the German version of Amadeus (Gottlieb) and even the odd saint's name thrown in for good measure. No, I am not being flippant—serendipitous, perhaps, particularly in my re-ordering of his names so that they tenuously relate to the themes by which I have chosen to head the sections of the book.

But enough of *Amadeus*, the present section, with its death-bicentenary connotations and the introductory nature of this part of the book. Let us change tempo and take up the baton again with *Wolfgang*.

WOLFGANG

He composed and speculated in the coach. His music needed no visual stimuli; it was self-contained; it followed its own laws and was not influenced by the appearance of the real sky above, whether fair or cloudy.

Alfred Einstein, 1944

Bars of Music—not Cages

One of my most valued friends, the late Christoph Lindenberg, a historian with remarkable insight and the author of a rororo best seller,[1] was once describing to me the soft spot (would passion be too strong a word?) he had for England, one which caused him to pay regular visits to the country over the years. It is some two or three decades ago and I can no longer quote him verbatim, but one of the things which drew him was to do with the *taming* influence of the ancient Arthurians[2] and the palpably lasting effect this had had on the landscape. Being a native, and at the time of our meeting a rather parochial stick-in-the-mud, I was surprised at what he said, not least because 'Arthur' was a long time ago, predating national monuments such as Westminster Abbey and the Tower of London. Moreover, this lasting effect he valued so highly was despite the concrete jungles that were rising in the cities and the spaghetti junctions that spawned increasingly across the motorway-ridden countryside. Of course, historian that he was, he referred to obvious phenomena like the love of the English for their gardens and the epitome of that love for and closeness to nature—the country village snug beside a gurgling stream, or a hamlet of clustered cottages hunched in Downland. But the influence went further than that. It was something that had entered into the very nature of the people: the decency on the roads to which the continental was so unaccustomed—I do not recall his referring to any incident which involved explicit vocabulary issuing from road rage!—the particular brand of diplomacy that he appreciated in British history, and so on. As he spoke, I curbed my urge to tuck my newspaper, with its headlines of the latest soccer hooliganism, under a settee cushion and inwardly settled for the attitude: Well if you say so ... But the idea of a culture being *tamed* lived on.

In former times in British circus rings with their snarling tigers and

---

[1] Christoph Lindenberg, 1975, *Waldorf-Schulen: Angstfrei lernen, selbstbewußt handeln*, rororo.

[2] A scholarly study of this period may be found in Richard Seddon, *The Mystery of Arthur at Tintagel*, Rudolf Steiner Press, 1990.

ominous-eyed pumas, the iron cage which appeared on the sawdust
during the interval into which the beasts prowled, and the full-
throated roars that filled the great marquee, left the onlooker in no
doubt about which side of the iron bars he was glad to be sitting on.
However, the crack of a circus whip is a mere tincture in the ocean of
culture. A tiger tamed in Moscow does not make the Malayan jungle a
safer place to be roaming in. But a culture—even the patchwork quilt
of fields and hedges was evidence for Lindenberg—tamed some
thousand years ago? That was something as enduring as Stonehenge or
the Prescelli mountains from which the monoliths are reputed to have
been transported for its construction. None of your overnight stops,
the big top flapping on high just in time for the crowds to come
trampling the grass, excited by a whiff of elephant dung foreign in the
nostril.

We can go twice as far back as Arthur. The sacred scriptures of
ancient Persia*, the civilization preceding that of ancient Egypt, from
whose source Zoroastrianism derives, reveal how a people were given
their task of taming nature for the purposes of husbandry: the transition of hunter-gatherers to cultivators. We do not normally think of
grains as tamed grass, though a dog's pedigree does not have to be a
one hundred per cent wolfhound for us to link the most domesticated
of animals with its wild progenitor. A cultural achievement indeed: the
reversal of traditionally one of the most rapacious predators of the
flock to that of its protector—or more precisely, and more to our
purpose here, the indispensable collaborator with the shepherd.

Does the Christian name Wolfgang suggest some such process in
Mozart's biographical development? The David in his soul-nature
felling the mighty Goliath? Some personal threshold Mozart had
crossed which materializes pictorially in the scene in *The Magic Flute*
when Tamino*, flute in hand, tames the beasts in the temple pre-
cincts? This problem has led many a biographer a merry dance,
especially if a large portion of the content of Mozart's extant letters is
included in the source material. The saints, so-called—many of
them—revealed traits in their characters which they took firmly in
hand and in doing so achieved the kind of inner development by
which their sainthood was acclaimed. Often, this inner process was
clothed by Medieval minds that had not lost the power of putting

truth in images, in such a way that they pictured the psychological drawback that impeded the saint's progress, and which had to be conquered, in the form of an animal. One only has to consider St Jerome and the lion, St Kevin and the blackbird, St Francis and the wolf of Gubbio, St Margaret and the dragon, and a dozen others to get onto the track of this line of thought. By contrast, Mozart's musical sainthood, let us call it, seems untouched by what could easily be mistaken for smuttiness of mind in his correspondence. Not only that, generosity and purity at several levels is frequently extolled in his everyday character. Were this not the case, his embarrassment at being seen in the company of the ill-mannered violinist Brunetti when they were obliged to attend on the Archbishop of Salzburg when he made his official visit to Vienna in March 1781, would be no more than the pot calling the kettle black. It would seem therefore that the unsavouriness which he displayed in an uninhibitedly childlike way—in fairly private circumstances, it should be stressed—has no bearing on his musicality, his musicianship, or his sublime musical achievements.

Any lengthy work on Mozart, of course, particularly to mark a biographical milestone such as the 250th anniversary of his birth, cannot ignore this fascinating yet problematic phenomenon of his Wolfgangishness. The course I am here adopting is to assume that, because such behaviour had so little apparently negative impact on his personal ethical standards or professional life, either the wolf never developed beyond the playful cub stage and therefore needed no taming, or it was merely some harmless residue having already been tamed somewhere, somehow, else; not wolves in a pack, but, if the mind can encompass and juggle with the idea, *lives* in a pack all bearing down on the Mozart incarnation. The foul-mouthed expressions in his personal correspondence are then no more than a hint of what lies in his and everyone's astral★ (or soul) nature and in no way mar the superb achievements of the Ego★. The kennel-less wolf cub in frolicsome perpetuity seems to have been perfectly at ease living its own innocuous life until the mastermind, having completed its ranging through the firmament of 'heavenly music', ordered the cub to heel, and was ready, meteor-like, to take time out and hurtle—albeit via the chandeliers, the laden larder shelves, the gaiters, garters and wig powder of earthly life—towards a quire of manuscript paper.

To investigate his style, therefore, I shall leave the mud-splattered road that zigzags round the mountain and make straight for the heights, familiar to both shepherd and sheep-dog alike. By abandoning the zigzag, however, I am not promising a sauntering climb. Before Tamino received Sarastro's blessing he not only had to tame the animals that oozed out of the shadows before the temple gateway, he had to undergo the tests which the priesthood imposed on him. These can come across as simplistic in the extreme, indeed completely fatuous in some productions of *The Magic Flute*, yet this need not prevent us from hearing a faint Sarastro-like echo of Zoroastrian mysteries at certain moments in the actual music.

Style and the Diatonic

We all liberally use the word *style*, and it is usually clear what we mean by it from the context, but the meanings are by no means identical. In fact they cover a wide spectrum. The question of style, therefore, is something of an open secret. The catalogue of Mozart's works, first drawn up by Köchel in 1862, lists over 600 compositions. Whatever it is, therefore, that constitutes style is visible to the eye and audible to the ear! It is sitting there on the music stand, plain for all to see. Yet until we either develop the eyes to see or the 'ears to hear' we remain blind and deaf to the open secret. Enjoying its fruits: yes abundantly. Understanding them and why they give us such spiritual nourishment: no, not yet.

Open secrets of this kind are also tantalizing, especially for those not content to put the mind at rest and simply listen, fumble towards several features of his music in a blind-man's-bluff's effort to grasp, and then to get a glimpse of, the grail of his open secret. But how far do we succeed? One person emphasises *genre* when they refer to style; another *mannerism*; a third will point knowledgeably to the kind of music that the composer is *emulating*; the *taste* that he is faithfully acknowledging or even pandering to with a particular audience in mind (Parisian, Viennese, Italian); a fourth will be content to rest on question-begging laurels (buffo, church, symphonic...); a fifth will point to finer details like the French preference (*goût*) for a minor episode before the rondo's★ return; a sixth will show how Mozart acknowledged his indebtedness specifically to the *Mannheim* orchestra under Stamitz and the traits which filtered into symphonic texture; a seventh will reveal the glorious fusion of *galant*★ *and learned* that Mozart increasingly achieves, and so on. All valuable in themselves, and each a jewel in the crown of Mozart's universality, but to what extent do they succeed in identifying the unmistakable voice of Mozartean authority; in placing him head and shoulders above the Salieris,★ Clementis and others of his minor contemporaries; in revealing him as the acropolis at the cross-roads between Haydn and Beethoven★—that style itself being the central continent in the vast ocean of Classicism between Baroque and Romantic?

Whilst we can safely leave Romanticism to be incubating, to understand Mozart we must first look at his pre-rococo ancestors. Baroque
music is the first mature child of the *diatonic*★ *system*. Though the post-
Renaissance child was conceived in the ardent minds of the prota-
gonists of *Le Nuove Musiche* (Florence 1602) in which the ideals of the
Camerata Fiorentina are presented in Caccini's 'Preface',[1] the style
that we recognize as Baroque matured in France, particularly at the
court of Louis XIV (1643–1715). From France it strode northwards
across the English Channel finding a welcome footing in the
Restoration compositions of John Blow★ and his pupil Henry Purcell.★ At the same time, like the rays implicit in the image of Le Roi
Soleil, it radiated north-east into the Netherlands, due east into what
became Germany, west into Spain and Portugal, as well as rebounding
across the Alps, back into the peninsular that was to become Italy, to
flourish there in the country's vast pre-Mozartean operatic output and
in the lyrical outpouring of instrumental music of which some of the
foremost representatives are Corelli, Vivaldi and Steffani★.

★ ★ ★

Some technicalities: the essence of Baroque style can be pinpointed to
what derives from the potential of the diatonic scale: C D E F G A B
(C).[2] One of the starting points for considering this potential is that it
has two equal tetrachords★—tone, tone, semitone; tone, tone, semitone.★ The so-called dorian mode[3] also has two equal tetrachords, but
the disposition of the tones and semitones is different, with the
semitone being at the bottom of each tetrachord. Thus the C scale,
with the *semitones at the top* of each tetrachord, follows a trend which
had been insinuating its way into music since the fifteenth century

---

[1] The Camerata consisted of a group of like-minded musicians (both amateur and
professional) meeting in the house of Giovanni de' Bardi, Count of Vernio in the
last quarter of the sixteenth century. Among the epoch-making ideals they
followed were: 'Only one melody should be sung at one time . . . and rhythm
and melody should follow carefully the manner of the speaking voice of
someone possessed of a certain affectation . . .' quoted by Claude V. Palisca in *The
New Grove*.
[2] I am here ignoring the conventional way of indicating different octaves such as
C_1 or c^{111}.
[3] E F G A B C D (E).

(through the use of *nota cambiata*★)—which ensured that a semitone gave a sense of focus as it rose to the *final*, for example, as in the final phrase of the well known folk-song 'Greensleeves'.

Focused tonality (a melody written in a diatonic scale whose melodic contour focused on its key note) led to doubly focused tonality through key contrasts and key relationships in the overall design—the upper tetrachord of the scale becoming the basis for the *dominant key*; the lower tetrachord of the scale becoming the basis for the *subdominant key*. Thus if the key of the piece is C major (with no sharps or flats), its dominant G major has one sharp and its subdominant F major has one flat. These two keys, it should be noted, have keynotes a fifth★ away from the original: going up: C D E F G and going down C B A G F. By logical extension to the still sharper and flatter keys, we arrive at two further scales in the diatonic system: D major with two sharps, B flat major with two flats, and so on.

Due to the (natural) tuning of instruments, Baroque composers seldom composed in keys whose *key signatures*★ went beyond scales that had more than four sharps or four flats.[4] But even when the various efforts to equalise the tuning of all 12 semitones into the octave resulted in *well-tempered* tuning,[5] the Baroque composer still retained a

---

[4] J.S. Bach provides momentary exceptions in the two famous Passions at cosmically tragic moments but these exceptions are not whole pieces. Mozart's early piano sonatas K279–284, written when he was 18–19 years old, are all in modest keys: C, F, B flat, E flat, G. D. The only number in *The Marriage of Figaro* with a key signature of four accidentals is Barbarina's aria in F minor. She sings it when she has lost the token that proves to be something of a pivot in Susanna's outwitting the Count and his lechery. Could the choice of F minor be Mozart's way of hinting that the opera, for all its entertainment, is a mirror for a humanity which has lost the plot?

[5] Bach's 1st book of 24 Preludes and Fugues, one in each of the 12 major and minor keys, dates from 1722. He uses the title *Das wohltemperierte Clavier*: 'equal temperament', where all 12 semitones are mathematically the same distance apart, took time to evolve. Rameau's prominence in this field (from 1735 onwards) points to the phenomenon as being one connected with the Intellectual Soul.

musical palette which ensured the double focusing of the tonic⋆ (centrally placed between a sharper and a flatter key),[6] thereby predisposing the tonal structure of the music. This *threefold key structure* of a central key between its sharper and flatter neighbours—together with the three so-called relative⋆ minor keys of each of the three—is evident in all Baroque genres: opera (which predominated in solo arias), Passion, oratorio, the overture, the prelude and fugue, the concerto, the trio sonata, the more descriptive pieces that poured so abundantly from the pens of the French composers, and the sonata as developed by Domenico Scarlatti at the Spanish court in Madrid.

Not only were the *key relationships*, which together with thematic material informed the *structure* of the music, determined by this potential within the diatonic scale. The *harmony* of the music beat by beat, bar by bar, was also informed by a 'system' of three plus three chords, the *triads*⋆ built on the notes of the scale (excluding the seventh degree in the major scale and the second degree in the minor scale, whose triads are neither major nor minor). The diagram is a visual representation of this.

White notes are major triads, black notes are minor triads.

The gallant style, which had superseded the Baroque, nevertheless retained the basic structure implicit in the diatonic system. What the Rococo gallant saw as the bath water of the Baroque—perhaps an inevitable and historically essential stage in the discovery of its own identity, like the adolescent leaving home—for once in the evolution of consciousness did not dispose of the baby as well. We will leave aside the nature of the mote in the Rococo eye that saw Bach as bath water (when the eye was bathed, of course, his music became the healing spring for which we all still thirst—for *bath* read *Bach*!) and proceed to the year of Mozart's birth, a quarter of a millennium ago.

---

[6] A bold exception is to be found in J.S. Bach's A flat major fugue in the second book of 'the 48', in which one entry is in the dominant minor.

Visiting—from Where?

Amongst the many pinch-of-salt anecdotes about Mozart, one of my favourites is the popularly traded one (from the picture postcard stand at the entrance to the tabernacle?) of the child prodigy skipping up to Marie Antoinette and embracing her uninhibitedly. The other image that rises beside this is from the painting dated 1790, portraying a late eighteenth century Austrian Lodge Masonic ritual, with Mozart in the foreground.[1] These two images, I would suggest, contain seeds of the truth not only of Mozart's journey in life but also of his musical style: the prince won his princess—that is, the soul became united with the higher self. With Mozart, however, there was mingling from the outset: original participation and final participation.[2] In more chivalrous times, a prince by blood still had to win his spurs; Edward the Black Prince at Crécy in 1346, or the sons of João I of Portugal at the battle of Cueta, the Moorish garrison and trade post on the southern side of the Straits of Gibraltar, in August 1415, come to mind as examples. Someone who composed three violin concertos while yet a teenager, concertos which are still the staple diet of the repertoire for solo violinists, and of audition requirements for the rank and file, didn't have to travel far from the cradle to find the spurs of destiny that had been awaiting the moment of his birth.

His life journey began in a musical household. Leopold however was more than an accomplished musician. He fathered Mozart both genetically and in his upbringing. While he provided the Ego principle for the early years (organizing the tours with Mozart and his sister Nannerl), at the same time he ensured that Mozart met the world—or at least the hubs that were at the centre of the wheels that conveyed the jolting carriage of Europe across its hummocky course in the second half of the eighteenth century.

---

[1] The painter is unknown. The painting is owned by the Historisches Museum in der Stadt Wien. See H.C. Robbins Landon, *Mozart and the Masons*, Thames and Hudson, 1982.

[2] See O. Barfield, *Saving the Appearances*, Faber and Faber 1957, Chapters VI and XX.

It was just before the beginning of Mozart's second septennial period that the first tour took place. Purely from the point of view of *archetypal* child development this clearly created a conflict. The etheric* body benefits from rhythm and regularity. Coach tours pace-wise, destination-wise, people-wise, time-wise, food-wise ... entail constant change. Mozart, however, contains more of the immortal *arche* than the earthly *typical* so we must try and assess the situation with that in mind. Nevertheless, we cannot escape the fact that so much juvenile limelight must have had an accelerating effect on an already precocious nature. Yet some balance was brought in: Leopold provided fatherly guidance, albeit somewhat jealously, that extended into the composer's adult life well beyond the norm. There is a further paradox: instead of the stable home life that youngsters thrive on, Mozart's experience for long stretches was one of being 'only a visitor' however fêted he was. Equally, stability was to evade him as an adult. Gold watches galore (if I may exaggerate) rather than daily bread and a secure position turned out to be his lot, yet it was a destiny imprint for the Ego—especially when that Ego was to inhabit the body for only 35 years. So we are faced with a career distinguished here and there, though nothing that forest-fired the imagination of his contemporaries *en masse*; a career which nonetheless left a mark whose post-mortal expansion was rapid. The memory of the visitor seemed more impressionable than the visitor himself.

Mozart is known to have had scarlet fever toward the close of his first septennial period. If the physical body is a symbol of earth, scarlet fever is an indication that the 'visitor' to the physical is more than the physical can cope with.[3] Thus a 'child study' approach to Mozart would suggest that the soul-spirit nature was considerably stronger than the physical and etheric. This was aggravated, as we have seen, by an irregular life from between the age of 6 and 17–18, with an emphasis on innate *genius* (spiritual gift) being constantly called upon and exposed to the influence of high ranking people in surroundings of grandiloquence. Might it even be that though posterity has been the heir to mature works from an early age (the three violin concertos

---

[3] See V. Bott, *Anthroposophical Medicine*, Rudolf Steiner Press 1978, p.92.

mentioned above, for instance) the maturity was somewhat at the cost of robust forces (cf. the longevity of Haydn)?

Be that as it may, from the beginning Mozart made his own distinct mark which, from a social point of view, culminated in his launching out freelance from the Archbishop of Salzburg's employ. We see him continuously absorbing the genres of his age and making them his own. Individuation on this scale is a conspicuous Ego phenomenon. Meanwhile, he teaches, responds to commissions however lofty or mundane but does not go the way of nature (cf. Haydn's *The Seasons, The Creation*). One is tempted to think that his music derives from a higher source than that which external nature can inspire (which is not to imply that the *composition technique* itself is superior). Notwithstanding, it would be naïve to suppose that that higher source had anything to do with the Church. The Salzburg experience in itself would suggest curtains down on mitres! Yet Mozart had an abiding love for the church organ, wrote masses and abhorred Voltaire's atheistic philosophy, for example. It seems more likely that he experienced the Divine—and simultaneously the fallen from the Divine—*in people*, as can be readily seen in *Idomineo*★ (a glance at the past), *Figaro,*★ *Don Giovanni,*★ and *Cosi fan Tutte*★ (the Mozartean present), and *The Magic Flute* (symbolic of the future).

It also seems self-evident that Freemasonry, which came at a significant moment into his life (1784), nourished and affirmed for him what was always there and, in view of his mature years and the outpouring of his genius into *The Magic Flute*—made the source of his inspiration more conscious. This also coheres with the fact that, although Haydn also became a Freemason, his non-attendance at the Lodge after his reception would suggest that he drew his inspiration from other sources.

Quill in Hand: Mind with Outstretched Wings

In his biography of Mozart,[1] Alfred Einstein comments on the 'impenetrable mystery' that Mozart's inner process of composition presents. Ultimately, that would seem inescapable, for any true mystery must, by definition, be at least unfathomable. However, it surely behoves those who wish to appreciate his genius, even in Dent's 'scientific' sense,[2] to *begin* to penetrate the mystery.

Starting at the end product, the legacy of his scores, we are given a more certain entry into the way his mind worked as a result of the research carried out into his often referred to musical handwriting. Through examining the two non-linked 'mechanical' yet rhythmical processes going on as he wrote an orchestral score—the quill full of ink giving out in the process of writing, and the quill becoming blunt and needing sharpening with a *penknife*—we know that he sketched out the whole movement of a symphony from A–Z, jumping grasshopper-like (yet with grasshopper sure-footedness) from one instrument's stave★ to another to indicate the seamless flow of the music phrase by phrase. After completing this, he returned to bar 1 and laboriously 'filled in' the notes and rests for all the other players. This means that most, if not all, of the *composing* had been brought to perfection in his mind beforehand and sitting down at his desk to write out the score, given perhaps the addition of a finishing touch here and there, was a mere process of transcription: transcribing what he heard with his 'mind's ear' into conventional signs and symbols that would enable other musicians to come along with their trumpets, double-basses and conductors' batons and recreate the sounds in performance.

The circumstantial evidence to support this journey of the music from Mozart's mind onto the manuscript paper is legendary. For instance:

---

[1] A. Einstein, *Mozart*, Cassell 1944, translated by A. Mendel and N. Broden, p.137.
[2] For Dent, see below.

(i) The overture to *Don Giovanni* was only written down after the dress rehearsal had taken place, leaving the copyist the unenviable task of writing out the parts during the rest of the night and the following day in time for curtain up. (One is even tempted to make the anecdote still more apocryphal and think that Mozart was, in fact, fashioning the final form of the composition in his quick-as-lightning mind *at the same time* as conducting the rehearsal!)

(ii) While the orchestra all had music to play from, the soloist's part for piano concertos was not always written down. To avoid plagiarism (or worse) he would play the piano part from memory.

(iii) Regarding the accompaniment to K454, the work he wrote for Strinasacchi the celebrated virtuoso violinist, he did not have sufficient time to write it out before the performance but simply sat down at the keyboard as she played, and accompanied her from memory.[3] Thus we have three different situations corroborating essentially the same mental feat. More could be cited.

The above indicates that Mozart must have had a) an incomparably all-encompassing mind to structure and retain a whole movement lasting several minutes (or more: a whole work) purely in the realm of thought, in considerable perfection too, since there are comparatively few corrections or false starts among his manuscripts; and b) a phenomenal musical memory, something, perhaps, akin to the memory of ancient minstrels transferred into relatively modern times. This is something that, admittedly, belongs to the domain of performing artists in the natural course of events, but in his case exceptionally so. Either side of the coin, actually, had its drawback. Not to be able to write the music down was a torment for him. Painstakingly writing it down could become a grinding chore for a mind that could work out the fugue while in the very act of transcribing the prelude, the mental equivalent, one can only imagine, of writer's cramp. As

---

[3] Regina Strinasacchi (1764–1839). It was in 1784 that the performance of his B flat sonata for violin and clavier took place. He expressed something of his admiration for her—by which we may also glean qualities that he valued highly in musicians: 'Her whole heart and soul are in the melody she is playing. No one can play an adagio with more feeling and more touchingly than she.' This helps to explain why the 1st movement of the sonata opens with an adagio of such outstanding majesty and beauty.

with many other great composers and other performers, we know that Mozart was a master at improvisation. When he described the way the clarinet sonata (composed on 22 October 1777) 'sprang out of my head', one gets the impression of a process that is a musical replica of Athena born as a fully mature adult—goddess, to be exact—from the forehead of Zeus.

★ ★ ★

We have evidence that his second thoughts, though these were not common occurrences, were simpler than his first. This would suggest that, by default, so to speak, his mind resided in or was able to piercingly tap into a realm that was spiritually fermenting—his proliferation of concerto themes thrown out in the opening orchestral ritornello★ is a neat indication of this—and that while one person might experience such a realm in, say, mathematical terms, Mozart was a channel for its musical manifestation. In order to discover the fountainhead of this, one is tempted to look in the direction of Plato's 'Musica Mundana' (Kepler's 'harmony of the spheres'), boundless, ceaselessly orbiting, paeaning the music of hierarchical beings. Looked at from that standpoint (albeit hardly *standing*), Mozart's task was to cool down an exhilarating lava-flow of cosmic sound into melody, harmony and rhythm. Small wonder that his music abounds with chromaticisms★ and that his themes are models of rhythmic fantasy, that on occasion could scarcely be crammed into the tiny closet of his contemporaries' powers of apprehension.

Yet herein (the contemporary scene and the temptation to force what can be experienced as the Osiris-radiance★ of his music into the Set-coffin of popularity) was one of his main dilemmas. It did not require Hoffmeister★ to make it clear that a popular style would have sold like hot cakes. But the last thing Mozart was willing to do was to compromise his art. The blue-pencilling of his letters may not have gone nearly far enough for fastidious eyes. That, tantalizing though it may be, is no more connected with the source of inspiration of his art than an eel sliming its slithery way amongst the rocks on which a lighthouse is constructed, is linked with the flashing light that has saved or ensured the safety of a thousand lives.

We see him struggling, nevertheless. His absorption of the gallant style which had insinuated itself into contemporary culture, though imprinted with his unfaltering genius, had some way to go in his estimation—that is, if his lifelong attention to polyphony is anything to go by. Would it be fair to say that he found the way to composition had jumped out of the frying pan of the platitudinous *figured bass*,★ into which mediocrity much Baroque had sunk, into the fire—a barely lukewarm fire—of threadbare gallantry, a situation he found completely abhorrent? Clementi's trifling speed antics at the keyboard were for him an example of the kind of cultural junk food that audiences were being fobbed off with. Like Cinderella's two ugly sisters, society could easily be beguiled with deceptions of art and Mozart was prepared to suffer (and did so right to his dying day) for his non-negotiable aesthetic principles.

The 'Hosanna' of the French Revolution's 'Liberty, Equality and Fraternity' relapsing into the 'Crucify' of the guillotine, was the tragedy of Paris. The potential tragedy of Vienna—footling rhythmical clichés, candy-coated melodies and pathetically bland harmonies becoming rife in popular taste—was not for him. But the full dignity of the threefold human being, something that stirred powerfully in the psyche of the Classicist, did not arrive handed on a plate. The left hand of the clavier first needed raising to the status of equal partnership with the right; the wind section in the orchestra first needed liberating so that each individual timbre could make its own voice heard; the cello needed liberating from its role of being slavishly tied to the figured bass; those at the heart of the orchestra or quartet (clarinet and viola, for example) needed liberating from the back seat of filling-in-obscurity and given independence.[4] All of this had to happen before the threefoldness of the music itself (melody, harmony, beat/rhythm) and of its instrumental grouping in the symphony orchestra, which, as we know it, became the Classical standard, was fully mature to sing the praises of evolving humanity *and* those of the one who pointed the forward way—Mozart.

---

[4] Apparently it was even some time after Mozart's birth that the clarinet 'arrived' in Salzburg; see F. Kerst, *Mozart: the Man and the Artist Revealed in his own Words*, Dover, 1965, translated by H. Krehbiel, p.7.

The Bohemians Understand Me

One of the reasons Rudolf Steiner gave for the study of the arts during teacher training was so that the teacher would gain a more acute perception of the child's 'higher' members through such a study.[1] The matter of higher members will be gone into in more detail in a later section. I raise the point here because of Mozart's uncanny access to the soul nature of the other person. Had he taken up teaching, other than to earn an honest and much needed penny for his family's daily life, there would certainly have been no one who could better his musicality—though we have yet to try and evaluate what might have been the significance of his visits to Padre Martini★ in Bologna in order to drill himself in counterpoint—and it is reasonable to suppose that his musicality would have transformed itself into a rare insight into the soul nature of his pupils. It is, however, on the stage, rather than in the schoolroom, that we find him inexhaustibly applying his skill. Mozart's astonishing ability to turn a sometimes not particularly engaging motif into a musical phrase—in other hands, it could be little more than a cliché—into a distinctive feature, *particularly* in the operatic ensembles where he excelled above all, has been commented on time after time. Amidst all the entanglement of the plot, we hear each individual's own stance as if we are looking at a portrait, and can see the wattles of an angrily outwitted minor official at court shake by the side of his double chin, or the suspicious frown contract on the brow of a duped husband, or the scarcely disguised wart suddenly displayed on the haughtily raised profile of an old harridan whose carefully calculated, minx-like composure has been saucily dented, and so on. Mozart's musicality gave him private access to all such psychological nuances that hid behind the convention, and enabled him, through an apt trill in the upper register of a clarinet, or a whole *string section*★ worrying away like a column of ants, or a deep staccato on the bassoon, or syncopated *sforzandi*★ on the French horn corrugating the musical texture to create a mood of confusion, etc., to

---

[1] See R. Steiner, *The Roots of Education*, 1968, Rudolf Steiner Press, Lecture 3.

depict a situation in the orchestral accompaniment that is correlative with what is being sung in the vocal line.

The same goes for the deeper aspects of the characters concerned. Mozart's sense of another's Ego[2] enabled him both to be adept in tinkering to good account with the libretti that came his way and to convey an atmosphere in an aria that gives the audience a grandstand view of each character's inner attitude, position in the social pecking order, moral stature and personal motivation, indeed a glimpse into their very heart-sanctuary. If *we* could only acquire an equivalent perception into Mozart's nature, as *he* had into that of Figaro, Osmin, Don Giovanni or Pamina,[3] the armour of Einstein's 'impenetrable mystery' might at the very least become a shade thinner.

★ ★ ★

It is known that as the family travelled in those early years the blinds of the coach were frequently drawn down. While the coachman must have been very much aware of the sulks and irritations of the horses, the vagaries of the weather, the grandeur (or awesomeness, terrifying to many an eighteenth century consciousness) of the mountains, Mozart and his fellow passengers were shoe-horned inside, jolted about on their plush seats, or made drowsy perhaps by the clippety-clop of hooves. We are talking here about long distances and long stretches of time. Turner was yet to come along and demonstrate how the eye of the beholder of nature could get closer to what she had to disclose if defying the warning of danger, the entire head and trunk were thrust out of a railway carriage window for nine minutes in a rainstorm.[4] We do not fully know to what extent Haydn imbibed what was 'out there', though his late masterpieces for solo voices, chorus and orchestra, *The Creation* and *The Seasons*, are a reasonable indication that his soul was not subject to the same taboo. For Mozart, Nature could be gently ridiculed (for example, the country bumpkin or Barbarina's father, the old gardener, in *The Marriage of Figaro*) but it could not be seriously thought of in the same breath as the ones who lorded it over Her.

---

[2] See W. Aeppli (no date) *The Care and Development of the Human Senses*, published by the Steiner Schools Fellowship.

[3] Characters from his operas.

[4] See G. Reynolds, *Turner*, Thames & Hudson, p.197.

Thus Mozart's reason for incarnating in Salzburg (to put it somewhat bizarrely) could certainly not have been to be close enough to
the Alps to enjoy the skiing! The travel agent and the *madness* of
getting away from it all were 'blessings' of the future. No. Mozart's
environment was culture, and culture meant people, the instigators of
it. He chatted to the grooms when finally, at the end of the 'stage', the
coach creaked and rumbled across the cobbled courtyard, came to a
halt and the door was flung open. He obliged Papa with his precocity.
With increasing resentfulness he obliged the crusty Archbishop
Hieronymous Colloredo. He wrote the oboe quartet K370 inspired
by the playing of the oboist Friedrich Ramm. He wrote the serenade
K375 for the sister-in-law of the court painter, and he personified
Mme Rose in the andante of one of his works. He responded to festive
occasions in the beer garden with *divertimenti*★. He responded to
instrumental virtuosi with *concerti*. He responded to the whims of
patrons in the salons, turning a blind eye no doubt on occasion to the
goings-on of the 'back stairs'.

Pearls before swine? Who can tell? And there is no need to become
judgemental here, but thankfully neither setbacks nor indifference
from a notoriously fickle public seemed to staunch the flow of
immortality. At least we know that he was appreciated in Prague.
More: 'The Bohemians understand me'. Or another flash through the
cloud blanket of impenetrability: 'Attwood *has got my style*'.[5] This is
loneliness. The frills, the laces, the fair or feigned finery of the courts
when he was fêted in childhood, and their counterpart in the Vienna
of the 1780s, all vanishing effervescence, like spring water poured out
at dinner when we know full well that the carbonated sparkles will
disappear and leave it flat before we are through our sirloin.

We should not, in all this, think that the one blest with genius is
necessarily aware of everything that is great in his *oeuvre*. Hans
Christian Andersen seemingly had little idea that his *Fairy Tales* would
be his lasting epitaph. Schubert might well have sacrificed a whole
portfolio of *lieder*★ to have an opera staged.

Another of my favourite images of Mozart is of him climbing into

---

[5] Thomas Attwood (1765–1838), English organist and composer who studied
with Mozart.

the organ lofts of places he visited and *standing* on the organ pedals because his legs had yet to grow long enough to allow him to play with his feet and sit on the organ stool at the same time. In this manner he revelled in the sound of the 'king of instruments' as he improvised. Yet the *thrill* of that favourite image is sobered by the fact that, despite his self-confessed need to procure a paid position, he turned down the possibility of becoming a fairly high-profile organist. We should not make too much of his kicking over the Salzburg traces and becoming freelance. His feet, even though now they could readily reach the pedals, needed to take him elsewhere. Seclusion, although it would have brought security, was not for him. Bruckner, one feels, was there to serve the far future; Mozart was a child of his time, the one who made the bridge between the great Haydn and Beethoven cantilevers of Classical culture. The ivory tower of ecclesiastical seclusion, especially the somewhat fake ivory of God's self-styled ministers as compared with the real thing, was too removed from the theatre, the market place, the bustle of crowds.

Yet here, too, Mozart's life and his pursuit of the *mean* brought him to an abyss. In 1782–83 Baron Gottfried van Swieten introduced him to the music of Bach. Bach, we could say, still 'lived in the sight of God' and the profundity of his music—evident as much in one of the fugues of 'the 48' as in the full glory of the Sanctus of the *B Minor Mass*—the sublime perfection of his counterpoint, the grandeur of his harmonic design achieved with a palette of only six keys, the banquet with which he could feast the soul derived from a musical motif consisting of only three consecutive notes of the scale (the Prelude in B flat minor of the first book of 'the 48'), the life which sprang from the seeds of his musical ideas when he tended them with the creative fantasy of his towering genius ... all of this was enough to bring even a Mozart to a temporary standstill. (The same happened to Haydn.) But it was not an inwardly inactive standstill. The meeting with Bach provided the inner alchemy that was to help convert the last traces of gallantic dross into the pure gold that comprised the crown of his last masterpieces, a phase launched, could one say, with the six string quartets dedicated to Haydn and culminating with the 'Jupiter' Symphony perhaps as the prize diadem in that crown.

The Bohemians, with Prague as their capital—Prague arguably still benefiting from the colourful aura of Rudolf II in Karlstein—were the people of middle Europe. Their central position between the technologically advancing West and the East with its historically endowed spiritual heirdom, clearly gave them an affinity with Mozart the composer whose understanding of the human soul stood somewhere between Shakespeare's and Verdi's. Just as indulgences had not been the only papal monstrosity that Luther* had swept away in favour of a renewed access to the Holy Book, so the Classicists needed renewed access to the 'Holy Book' of polyphony, but newly translated, so to speak, to be in tune with contemporary consciousness. Hence, before the Industrial Revolution, and before the children of Newtonian-like thinking could infiltrate every nook and cranny of culture, that thinking needed an injection of spiritual intensity to help provide at least the potential for balance. The heart, the regent of the 'middle man', was the best place for this intelligence, and Mozart evolved a style which went straight to the heart. The French had injected Europe with the Enlightenment (if enlightenment is what its outcomes in the metric system and all the rest of it truly was) but it was the Viennese, to and from whom the arteries and veins of so much of Central European culture flowed, who provided the heart. And with compass needle deflecting from Vienna to Prague as far as music is concerned, Mozart proved to be king of hearts.

Mozartean Integrity

There are essentially two ways of being a bad king: you listen too much to your people, or you listen too little. Henry VI[1] was driven hither and thither—eventually to his unhappy end—by leaning too readily on the opposing factions amongst his nobles. At the other end of the scale, Richard II was deaf to Gaunt's timely warning that his egotistically riotous ways were putting his crown in jeopardy. Apart from the later play Henry VIII, Shakespeare's histories lead to the climax of Henry V. On his accession, his tippling with the lads instantly ceased, yet he still walked the camp at night at Agincourt to listen to the voice of the people, later, good-humouredly commending honest outspokenness.[2] At the same time, his leadership was legion. Without his contagious enthusiasm 'for England and St George' the bedraggled English bowmen would surely never have pulled it off.

Although Mozart's popular success seems to have come with *The Marriage of Figaro* in 1786, his own evaluation was that K452, for oboe, clarinet, horn, bassoon and piano, (composed in March 1784) was his 'best work'. One wonders who might have spotted this in a modern radio-sponsored poll had Mozart not obliged us by already divulging the secret himself?! Regarding certain traits in the work, which were superb achievements if we bear in mind that the three upper wind instruments (oboe, clarinet and horn) are completely independent of the keyboard, and even more significant, the bassoon is free from the bass of the piano part, Mozart is not unique in such Classical achievements in the genre of instrumental music. Maybe one of his sources of pride in K452 was the fusion he achieved between gallant and learned styles, but let us leave that on one side in favour of identifying other outstanding traits, limiting our enquiry, for practical reasons, to the middle (slow) movement (see Appendix A).

---

[1] The following are brief references to Shakespeare's plays about early English monarchs.

[2] The good-natured exchange between Williams and Henry in Act IV, Sc.viii.

Here we find two unmistakable hallmarks of Mozart's style in the development★ section. The first is a theme played on the French horn as yet unheard. The horn takes its time, even considering the pace is already *larghetto* (using 6 of the 29 bars of the development—51–57). Furthermore, within the tonal design, the theme reclines as cushioned as could be in the subdominant key, with the *harmonic rhythm*★ at the beginning of each of its two phrases lasting for a full two bars. From the resultant laid-back mood we are ushered into one of extraordinary intensity (the second hallmark), following immediately on the horn's heels. It is a passage of 15 bars length with the key changing restlessly bar by bar, through the chords D_7★ - G_7 - B flat$_7$ - German sixth - g6/4★- E flat$_7$ - C_7 (*forte*) - e 6/4 (*piano*) - dim$_7$ - C 6/4 - dim7 - d 6/4 - dim 7 - [B flat 6/4 - F_7], followed finally by the recapitulation★ at bar 47. Thus Mozart gives himself only two bars (see square brackets) to return to the home key from no man's land, a territory made more disorientating through its dynamic hide-and-seeks. Did ever prodigal son tramp homeward with more fervour, more anguished determination?

Without going overly into detail, one could cite other characteristic features: (i) the inversion★ of bar 3's *forte descending* quavers transformed at the beginning of the development into *piano ascending* quavers; (ii) the frequent *alternation of piano and forte* of the opening theme, which goes on for a full 18 bars; (iii) the plaintive *chromatic* chords in the exposition (bars 28–30), that same harmony, changing at the quaver, which is then *extended for no less than another 8 bars* in the recapitulation (101–108); (iv) the development★ (bars 44–73) combining essentially *new thematic material* albeit some of it transformed as already noted from a subsidiary motif earlier in the work; (v) the whole of the second subject group★ *redefined* (cf. bars 36–44 and 113–124); (vi) *the final cadence marked with sudden piano* (123–124).

Mozart professedly had no desire to be original, notwithstanding, one wonders how he contemplated avoiding being utterly beacon-like Mozartean! To us, 250 years after the event, it would be tantamount to trying to tuck the Matterhorn imperceptibly away into some corner of the Cotswolds or into the Mississippi delta! The only possible interpretation is that he happily absorbed all genres, keeping consistent within them (opera distinct from mass; concerto distinct from symphony; song distinct from aria; sonata distinct from fantasia; quartet distinct from divertimento and so on) *without* the style that he had uniquely to bestow on humanity's evolving consciousness being cramped or hamstrung in any way. At the same time, one is inclined to think that his frequent harmonic boldness in various genres must have had at least some of its roots in the fact that he had been brought up on the keyboard, another obvious pointer in this direction being the piano concertos—almost in a category of their own in the repertoire.

We can thus far identify a fair handful of characteristic Mozartisms:
- elegant melodic lines—the *sine qua non* of grace,
- chromaticisms even when writing at breakneck speed,
- unity of style throughout each work,
- unfailingly exquisite craftsmanship,
- rich harmonic texture,
- recapitulations that always have touches of innovative musical fantasy up their sleeve,
- short but telling development sections,
- a profusion of rhythmically distinct thematic material,
- subtly balanced phrase lengths,
- a penchant for daring modulation,★
- an idiom which, even when portraying 'the folk', essentially steers clear of anything appertaining to folk art,
- speaking the (albeit gradually acquired) language of polyphony like a native,
- contrasts of every imaginable kind,
- gaiety alongside profundity—a contrast that deserves special mention,
- a light touch that nevertheless avoids trespassing on the ground of triviality,
- mastery of form even when highly unconventional,
- a prodigious facility in developing, extending and transforming thematic material.

Feed all that into a computer which contains Mozart's complete works in its memory and instruct it to compose symphony no. 42 and what would happen? Given a modicum of computer imagination, my guess is that the computer would say it had other things to be getting on with and hide its head in a large Boolean* dune of drifting sand! But why? Firstly because, despite all the information, we have not yet defined (if 'defined' is the right word) the exact nature of Mozart's *style*, running as a golden thread through the different genres in which he excelled and through the chromaticisms, the elegant phraseology, the joy-to-be-alive gaiety beside the profound commentary on it, and all the other above-noted Mozartean characteristics. And secondly because we have hardly yet alluded to how that golden thread fits into the fabric of humanity's evolving consciousness. It seems appropriate to baptize this aspect of Mozart's contribution as *Chrysostom*.

CHRYSOSTOM

[T]here was no getting out of the centenary: something had to be done . . .
He came at the end of a development, not at the beginning of one; and although
there are operas and symphonies, and even pianoforte sonatas and pages of
instrumental scoring of his, on which you can put your finger and say, 'Here is
final perfection in this manner, and nobody, whatever his genius may be, will
ever get a step further on these lines,' you cannot say, 'Here is an entirely new
vein of musical art' . . . Anybody, almost, can make a beginning: the difficulty
is to make an end—to do what cannot be bettered . . . 9 December 1891[1]

[Those who for years] have known Mozart only by vapid and superficial
performances . . . have hardly got out of the habit of regarding [his music] as
tuneful little trifles fit only for persons of the simplest tastes . . . 16 March 1892

With Mozart you are safe from inebriety. Hurry, excitement, eagerness, loss of
consideration, are to him purely comic or vicious states of mind: he gives us
Monostratos and the Queen of the Night on the stage, but not in his chamber
music . . . The true Parnassian air acts on these people like oxygen on a mouse:
it first excites them and then kills them. Give me the artist who breathes it like a
native, and goes about his work in it as quietly as a common man goes about his
ordinary business. Mozart did so . . . 19 April 1893

Shaw, Music in London

---

[1] This and the following two quotes are from George Bernard Shaw, *Music in London, 1890–1894*, 1931, Constable & Co.

Ancient Civilizations and Modern Consciousness

Re-reading Alfred Einstein's seminal study of Mozart, which appeared just before the bicentenary of the composer's birth,[1] I was struck by a point he makes in his concluding chapter: 'The definitive work on Mozart's effect on musical history has not yet been written'. Was Einstein, I wondered, despite all his unprecedented painstaking, barking up the wrong tree? Perhaps 'tree' takes the metaphor too far. My Israeli friends tell me that the olive, through growing to the age it so often does, gets handed down from generation to generation amongst the rurally inclined Arabs, not simply as olive grove by olive grove, or even tree by tree, but branch by branch. One son inherits one branch, another another. Passing through olive groves in the moonlight, when the clouds of dust have settled, and the crunch and clatter of the working day is carpeted with silence and the silver-drenched olive leaves gently canopying their ancient trunks imprint their moon-filled magic on the gnarled stillness, what foreigner to that culture would guess that each plant is, as like as not, a living replica of a family tree as well as the bearer of the precious fruit that has provided subsistence for that family perhaps over centuries? This evocative image, and Einstein's teasing remark, prompted the question: Is there not some important aspect of Mozart's work to which we have hitherto been oblivious?

Not completely, of course, yet as long as we are intent on barking up the purely biographical and musical branches of the Mozartean olive tree, I do not believe that we are likely to approach the kind of definitiveness that Einstein had in mind. I am certainly not claiming to be aiming at achieving the last word in this. Nevertheless, a woof woof or two beneath one of the other branches might open up useful prospects for future generations, music lovers 'n' all. One did not have to be an architect to benefit from the beauty of the proportions and form of a Greek temple. Even Mozart's contemporaries, the geniuses Goethe* and Schiller*, still saw, and were inspired by, Greece as the

---

[1] 1944, English edition 1946.

acme of beauty. Is there not something we drink in beneficially when listening to Mozart's music (always provided that we are reasonably attentive), that something being irrespective of our musical knowledge, ability or preferred taste?

To investigate what I have increasingly come to view as a somewhat overlooked aspect of Mozart's music (a forgotten or at least elusive olive branch) I am entering into Rudolf Steiner's portrayal of human nature, particularly those members which he links in one way or another with music. Not directly to understand the enigma of Mozart the man in the street beside Mozart the sublime genius both wearing the same shoe buckles, but from the higher perspective of when he incarnated. To do this, we shall need to place what Steiner refers to as Ego, Soul and Intellectual Soul at the centre of our enquiry. But to arrive there, first some anthroposophical★ 'basics'.

In clarifying the intricate and complex nature of the human being, Steiner first distinguished three 'organizations', let us call them, which he termed *physical, etheric and astral*. The *physical* can be thought of as the familiar 'flesh and bones' we carry around—that which casts its long shadow across the common as we walk the dog on a golden summer evening; or the immersed leg of famed density (not overlooking all the rest of the anatomy) which was the measurable partner of Archimedes' 'Eureka' realization; or that space-taking 'object' that costs us the price of a seat if we want to give our flagging soul and spirit a treat at the opera. The *etheric* we experience as the energies of life that sustain and nurture the physical from conception onwards, more like the source of strength within, with its ebb and flow of health and illness, or simply of being off colour one day and on top of the world the next. The *astral* organization is the seat of those activities in which we are involved, of which we are very much aware during our waking hours, and which common parlance refers to as our faculty of thought, our flow of feeling and our will-power. The two last (etheric and astral) dovetail with the first, needless to say: else part of us would be disembodied! The etheric has its physical counterpart in the rhythmic flow of the lymphatic system. The astral's tripartite 'intelligences' are also reflected in the physical: the nerve-sense system of the body provides the instrument used by our thinking activity; the respiratory/

circulatory systems affect and are affected by the life of feeling; whereas closest to and supporting and enabling willing to make itself effective are the metabolic and limb systems.

These three organizations (physical, etheric and astral) provide the foundation for further human members to evolve, this being possible through their having been brought to a comparative state of perfection in human development already as long ago as c. 3000 BC.[2] At that point, the individuality (the Self or Ego) of the human being, that principle which purely animal species do not enjoy, began to engender further members. These are of a purely metaphysical nature. In Steiner's terms, they manifest as different nuances of soul: a reactive nuance (the *Sentient Soul*), a more premeditated, sharply aware nuance (the *Intellectual Soul*), and a nuance in which the soul seeks to plumb the depths of physical existence with its effect on and potential outcomes for human life (the *Spiritual* or *Consciousness Soul*).[3] We are always drawing on and giving expression to all three of these members but with varying emphases. Two common or garden examples, the first rather irreverent, I suspect:

(i) The Sentient Soul might be the cause of our overdoing it at a party. The Intellectual Soul, startled, perhaps, on seeing what is reflected in the mirror the next morning as the regrettably visible effect of this, or on coming to terms with the inner effects through the haze of a headache (over black coffee!), brings us to our senses. The Consciousness Soul, pondering further, settles for going steady on the alcohol at future parties. (Notwithstanding, it still has to reckon with the desire of the Sentient Soul next time the 'bubbly' starts bubbling!)

(ii) We are thrilled to chatter point to hit upon a piece of knowledge in our research to which we have hitherto been blind (the Sentient Soul's immediate reaction). We dive into the relevant bibliography and invade the internet, amassing facts (the Intellectual Soul's more measured response, albeit driven by enthusiasm). We sift through the data, and consider and develop our conclusions, eventually consigning

---

[2] See R. Steiner, *Rosicrucian Wisdom, An Introduction*, Lecture 11, Rudolf Steiner Press, 2000.
[3] Known in German as: *Empfindungs Seele, Gemüt Seele, Bewußtseins Seele*.

them to print (the Consciousness Soul's further massaging of our findings).

Without ceasing, however, through all the millennia in which these members have been and are evolving, that which singles out the human being from the other 'kingdoms' of nature (mineral, plant, animal) a *conscious state of mind*—the Ego presence—prevails and presides, evolves, manifests, directs and bears the burden of holding the balance.

★ ★ ★

Obviously, all of this does not happen overnight. Even a brief glimpse at the centuries needed for the ascent, the prolonged poise at the summit and the subsequent decline of the major civilizations throughout history will give some indication of the stretches of time involved. Unlike outer nature, however, when seasonal flow, despite the wonder it may evoke, seems like an inexorable turning of the cycle of the year, human evolution is a constant fount of new developments. To examine a part of it, one star in the firmament of evolution as high at the zenith as we care to direct our gaze—*Mozart's style*—we need to attune ourselves both to the blink of evolutionary time in which his star flashed forth, and also keep track of how that moment relates to the vast time scale of the past stretching through the present into the future. Awesome, perhaps, mind-stretching certainly, but we would do well to bear in mind that awe was known to the Greeks as the gateway to wisdom, and that the mind, if Mozart is anyone to go by, ultimately knows no bounds.

Steiner described the development of consciousness of humanity not only in terms of what can be seen, what was achieved as the external product of people's inner life, *vis-à-vis* the principle civilizations on earth, but taking those achievements as empirical evidence he sought to characterize the prevailing consciousness that was the generating factor for all outer manifestations. Such civilizations, of course, can be found across all continents. He chose, however, to give a certain emphasis to the sequence of civilizations which leads from the Far East to present day Europe (the setting for Mozart's work), arriving there via the ancient civilizations of Persia, Egypt, Greece and Rome. Parallels in other parts of the world can be, and have, of course, been richly identified by the anthropologist. In Steiner's view, each civilization reflected in its outer life, in its artefacts, traditions and inventions, as well as in its beliefs and rituals, the process of evolution in consciousness which was taking place *through* its people—what virtually amounts to its mission, irrespective of the degree to which that mission was being consciously pursued. But in comparison to those classifications such as we find in the terms Stone Age, Iron Age or Bronze Age, Steiner was not content simply to designate such civilizations by referring to their most characteristic outer circumstances or achievements, however justified, typical and illuminating that may be. He epitomized the achievement of each civilization by identifying the *member* of the human being generated—that which was particularly under the cosmic spotlight, so to speak, as well as by going in substantial and significant detail into the nature of each civilization, together with its corresponding member, to elaborate his point. These members, apart from the physical body itself, are, of course by definition metaphysical. Hence the juxtaposition of *spiritual* and *science* in Steiner's whole world outlook and the emphasis he placed on the central part played in evolution by the human being, as revealed in the word (though he did not coin it) by which that world outlook is most often designated: *anthroposophy*.

In this context, and crucial for our present study, is that (metaphysical) member which resulted from the epoch of Ancient Greece, Rome and the Middle Ages, which formed the back drop for what is presently in the foreground of evolution, the 'Western' age. As already touched on, he termed that member the *Mind Soul* or *Intellectual Soul*, and described how it underwent a cosmically necessary process of recapitulation, largely in the seventeenth century, before the characteristics of the present age could begin freely to unfold. This provides us with a fairly high-powered lens for considering Baroque musical style, the inception of which occurred mainly in France, as the precursor to Viennese Classicism, of which Mozart, our present maestro, might be considered the central figure. Central if, of the three who towered far above all others, we generally accord Haydn the honour of being the main pioneer of the style and Beethoven as the one who led Classicism through the broadening estuary of his personal and impelling powers towards the expectant ocean of Romanticism.

The Past Recapitulated at the Outset of Our Modern Epoch

For many it will come as an eyebrow-raiser when they first hear that Rudolf Steiner pointed to the year 1413 as that in which the present age began. Two years before the bowman's arrow sped through the air at the Battle of Agincourt seems a long way from a trip to the moon, or the casual attitude into which we can find our media-fatigued selves subsiding when hearing of the latest suicide attack in Baghdad. Viewed, however, from the point of view of what the Consciousness Soul has to achieve and the preparation for this over aeons, it is easier to see that year in its geo-cosmic perspective rather than trying to cram it mentally into the midst of nappy changing or when we find ourselves without an umbrella on a showery April afternoon.

In any case, before the development of the Consciousness Soul could get underway, a process of recapitulation had to take place. Those soul qualities—referred to as the Sentient Soul and the Intellectual Soul—with which the human being had been endowed through the cultural achievements of the ancient Egyptians and the ancient Greeks, had first to be re-experienced in the context of the new age. In his early educational work Steiner draws our attention to those peoples who had this task. In Renaissance times the Italians (Spaniards too) re-embodied, so to say, the Sentient Soul; while in the seventeenth century the French spurred the Intellectual Soul into its modern setting.[1]

Looking for manifestations of this in music, we have a wealth of compositions from Renaissance Italy (for many, a 'golden age' whose rays warmed all European climes), and from the Baroque (when the French Court of Louis XIV was acknowledged in so many respects as the high point of *culture*). By contrast, it has to be admitted that we cannot easily examine their counterparts in ancient Egyptian and Greek times. At least, not in the same medium of music. Though the

---

[1] See R. Steiner, essay, 1927 (with numerous later impressions), *The Education of the Child in the Light of Spiritual Science*, Rudolf Steiner Press.

mystery of the pyramids is only gradually being unveiled, their structure remains largely intact, alongside many other archaeological features from the age. From the vast treasury of those monumental remains we can get beyond many of the approximations we are forced to settle with for some cultures, and begin to reconstruct the original. Similarly with Greece, despite the disastrously ravaging years that have intervened. With such aspects of ancient civilizations, it is only a matter of the mind advancing far enough to gain insight from the archaeological relics and other remaining artefacts into what aspect of human consciousness gave rise to the phenomena that have come down to posterity. But while there is much for the eye that broadly indicates various aspects of *the place that music held* in those far-off societies, there is nothing of comparative value for the ear. However informed we may be at surmising, and however intuitive, we cannot *hear* what Egyptian and Greek ears heard, still less experience how their music instilled, engendered, prompted or affirmed their two respective soul qualities: Sentient and Intellectual Souls.

The lack of sufficient musical evidence, however, does not bar us from forming *ideas* of their soul qualities. Put in a very compact nutshell—the kernel of which could easily be expanded into the size that the germinating beans grew to in 'Jack the Giant Killer'—the soul in Egypt, seen archetypally, was endeavouring to connect its rich spiritual inateness with earthly life. The land itself, in the valley of the Nile, was confined on both sides of the river. The south–north flow of the Nile, with its annual, life-bringing film of fertile alluvium washing over the land, was straight-jacketed, as it were, in granite. As the temples began to be built into the erstwhile prohibitive face of those granitic outcrops,[2] the soul sent down the roots of its rich cosmic experience into earthly existence. Roots that were more like the long, water-seeking tap root of the date palm than the spreading outreach, say, of an oak's or laburnum's root systems. So motivated were the Egyptians to connect with the earth, that they even delayed the full entrance of the departing soul-spirit into the spiritual world after death. The elaborately mummified bodies, so central a feature of their culture, bear witness to this. To borrow an image from geology, it was

---

[2] See G. Richter, *Art and Human Consciousness*, 1985, Anthroposophic Press.

as if they valued the stalagmites that raised themselves from the ground beneath the cosmic vault of their cultural heritage more than the stalactites that represented the spirituality that seeped bountifully with star wisdom into the splendour of dynasty following dynasty, as well as into every corner of their daily lives.

For the Greeks, the emphasis lay elsewhere. The archipelago of Greek islands affords us an image, not of a straight-jacket, but of a culture that was much more out in the open. With temples on promontories, or at the focal centre of wide arable plains, which, even though an air of secluded sanctuary often surrounded them, celebrated the vitality of being alive. From the etheric, the hand-in-glove companion of the physical body, flowed the energy for their sculptures, their education and many other aspects of cultural, political and daily life. And in the realm of the mind the same vitality worked, through philosophizing, to *make sense* of all that surrounded them. In their sun-filled cosmic-earthly existence, it was nevertheless the earthly plane where they became essentially at ease; in this sense they were heirs to Egypt. Despite the huge panorama of Greek mythology, the world of spirit (from which those cultural stalactites had descended in Egypt) was already distancing itself from their consciousness. For the Greek, it was 'better to be a beggar on earth than a king' in that other world, 'the land of shades', with its chilling, deathly connotations.

★ ★ ★

However, although from the time of Egypt to that of Greece humanity had clearly stepped across one of its major cultural thresholds, the *mood* of people's consciousness in musical terms could be said to be still encompassed within that of the fifth.[3] That is, the spiritual world, albeit in different degrees, still remained a vital factor in the equation of human experience. For Steiner, the *mood of the fifth* denotes the quality of consciousness of humanity that pervaded all the first four Post-Atlantean★ epochs, that is until the year mentioned earlier, AD 1413, from which point a significant change in consciousness became apparent—apparent, that is, if one looks at the

---

[3] See R. Steiner, *The Inner Nature of Music and the Experience of Tone*, 1983, Anthroposophic Press.

decade and century hands of the clock, rather than those of the minutes and hours. This change he characterized by a similar musically half-technical expression, *the mood of the third*. Even the use of thirds (and their inversion, sixths) was slow to insinuate itself into music at this time of transition from the fourth to the fifth Post-Atlantean epochs. The so-called Chartres manuscript, dating from as early as the eleventh century, and discovered in the twentieth, would indicate that free organum, which clung essentially to unison, octave, fifth and fourth (the latter sometimes extended beyond the octave) in the intervals created 'between' its two voices, was on the cusp of this change of consciousness as Gothic was about to spread from its major inception in Chartres to other parts of the West. Celtic (Welsh) manuscripts from the Middle Ages, too, would suggest that their music also induced more inwardness (the characteristic of the mood of the third) than that of other European peoples, though it is not a straightforward matter to reconcile this with the traditional view that Celtic consciousness had retained a certain freedom from becoming bound to the world of outer sensory perception. The reconciling can be helped, perhaps, on realizing that Chartres (known earlier as Carnutum) is situated in Normandy, i.e. where Norse and Celt intermingled.

The threads of how the interval (and hence the mood) of the third filtered into Medieval music are fine. Here we need only acknowledge that in the music of Renaissance Italy—and we may take that of Palestrina★ to be the pinnacle of so-called sixteenth century style—those threads were fully woven into the style that prevailed. At the same time, their fineness meant that the resultant fabric still had an overall quality in which the mood of the fifth lingered on from the past. Features that corroborate this are not difficult to identify. The music was pre-diatonic and thus had no key structure. The scales were modal★ without a sense of tonic finality (despite what was designated as the 'final') to anchor them with a quality of firm Ego-centricity. The majority of compositions were conceived polyphonically with melodic lines for each musician that were redolent of the other worldliness of Gregorian plainchant. The entries★ of the different voices were at the unison, octave, fifth or fourth—intervals that to this day we still classify in the theory of music as *perfect* intervals. In the chords that resulted from the interweaving melodic lines, it is mostly the root★ or the fifth that is 'doubled'. The association of beat and barline is a thing of the future.

Hence, just as in Egypt the tap root into earthly consciousness was being sent down, the *use* of the third in the pure Renaissance style, however modest, had definitely 'come to stay'. In Egypt, we find the soul, while still primarily flooded with awareness of the spirit, eager to respond to earthly circumstances: as we have seen, as the huge endeavour necessary to provide sustenance for daily life from a land whose fertility was dependent annually on the flooding waters of the Nile; in the use of the hardest of earth's minerals in its structures and monuments, in massive quantities and dimensions, with all that that entails; and at the termination of earthly life with the death of the physical body, the soul's extended post-mortal connection with the earthly sphere through the mummifying of the body; and so on. All this is echoed in the use of the third in the harmony of Renaissance music. Yet the lingering adherence to Medieval modes endows it with a sublime air of other worldliness, a palpable quality that can as well be experienced by a motet group getting together in the brashest of modern apartments, as by a professional choir singing in the sacramental setting of a Gothic cathedral with its not-quite-of-the-earth acoustics.

Between Baroque and Romanticism

With the change from music based on those modes to that based on the diatonic scale came all the features of tonal music that we associate, albeit progressively, with the Baroque, Classical and Romantic styles. In that the Baroque style emanated particularly from mid-seventeenth century France, we are concerned here with its connection with the Intellectual Soul as a recapitulatory manifestation of the original begetting of that Soul quality in ancient Greece.

All the potential which is inherent in the diatonic scale itself gives us the clue. A brief recap: the two tetrachords of the scale are identical as far as the patterns of their intervals is concerned,[1] as well as having the semitone between the third and fourth notes. The sharpened *leading note*★ gives finality to the octave—it reaffirms the tonic. This, together with the corresponding other two tonics, that of the 'sharper' key based on the dominant and that of the 'flatter' key based on the sub-dominant, and together with the three so-called relative minor keys (with tonics on the sub-mediant, the mediant and the super-tonic) provides the basis for the whole of the tonal system. The freedom of modulation which results from these two 'equal' tetrachords also serves the affirmation of the home key when, the music having gone on its tonal journey, the final return to that home key comes about. All this reflects the feeling of firm confidence that the Greek enjoyed as far as the incarnation of the Ego into its (earthly) sheaths is concerned. We see that confidence in the way the Greeks revelled in the sheer beauty of the physical body, by which they represented their most revered gods and goddesses in the sculptures which abounded in their temples and in the mythological aspects of their spiritual-cultural life. And back it surges in the incessant satisfaction that the Intellectual Soul derived from Baroque tonality with its constant reference to the home key and with all other key relationships providing the musical perspective necessary. On the one hand, the harmonic tonal pattern of Baroque music kept fairly faithfully to its six chords and corresponding six keys

---

[1] Rising tone tone semitone.

(a City State similarity, in which Thebes, Sparta, Athens, etc. had its own quality while still retaining an overall Greek identity?); on the other hand, the fluidic ease with which those six chords, or even key-hints, featured, kept the danger of tonic-imprisonment at bay (the effervescent spirituality of the Greek Intellectual Soul?). The fluidic ease, however, is not allowed to become wildly random. The balance of the sixfoldness as an orbiting experience around the home tonic is maintained, the indefatigable pursuit of which provided the Intellectual Soul emanating from Baroque France with invigorating possibilities.

Rudolf Steiner commented on the remarkable ability of the Greek sculptor to portray movement[2]—battle scenes between gods and centaurs, the charioteer with his horses galloping at full tilt, athletes in action, eurythmic dancers, the oceanic play of dolphins around Poseidon, the thunderbolt of Zeus about to be hurled across the heavens, Pluto abducting Persephone, Hercules superhumanly engaged in his mammoth trials, the three figures in the Laocoön wrestling with the death-dealing serpents, and a thousand others—movement exulting in bodily freedom, but in such a way that the beholder nevertheless experiences *inner balance*. The Baroque composer achieved that quality of movement in balance through constantly changing the harmonic perspective (not tonal), triad by triad, so that we view the stability of the home key through a kaleidoscope of sharper and flatter chords and through relative major and minor chords. As the music progresses through time, it is as if we hear what the Greek experienced in the figures comprising the frieze along the sides of the temple. The cine-camera is a modern extension, some would say, travesty, of this, though this is not to decry the art of film-making.

We find the quality again, for some modern tastes even to excess, in Baroque architecture and, what we are primarily concerned with here, in other aspects of Baroque music. Even a cursory glance at the bass line, with its ever-flowing, often restless momentum reveals this,[3] as

---

[2] See R. Steiner, lectures on the history of art in 1916–1917, not published in English.

[3] The Baroque bassoonist must have had exceptionally capacious lungs to cope!

well as the tireless figuration reminiscent of the coming of spring, the ubiquitous grace notes★ fluttering through the musical phrases like aspen leaves, the grand cycles and epicycles of keys in the tonal design of the larger ritornello-like movements, and the mental acrobatics of imitation, sequences,★ inversions, diminutions, etc., in the virtuosic display of counterpoint in the work of some of the most eminent of the Baroque composers. Small wonder that the end of such a piece needs no final IV–V–I cadences to emphasize the close in a Rossini★-like way. Just as the Greek Intellectual Soul—born of the etheric, with the Ego as midwife—portrayed movement brought through harmonious balance into sculptured rest, so the Baroque composers brought the cosmic whirring of their basic tonal sixfoldness into a state of musical equilibrium with the final note/chord of the movement—no more, no less.

The world of inspiration from which true Baroque music flows, being packed into the comparative confines of six mathematically straightforward and interrelated diatonic key relationships, thus advances the Greek Intellectual Soul into the modern era. Whereas Greek consciousness was in the mood of the fifth, the style of Baroque music clearly derives from mood-of-the-third consciousness. Furthermore, in Baroque style we experience 'mood of the third' through the overriding principle that the hearer must experience the Ego-centring of the opening of each movement affirmed at the end. Not through keynote★ thumping insistence, but through musically symmetrical balance; major and minor in balance (irrespective of whether the home key *is* major or minor); through the principle thematic material and its complementary episodes★ being in balance, and, above all, through the experience of the sharper keys (the dominant with its relative minor) and flatter keys (the sub-dominant with its relative minor) held in balance through *their* centre, the key that bears the key signature of the piece.[4] A Star of David (two intersecting equilateral triangles, one apex pointing upwards, one downwards) comes to mind as a visual symbol of this.

Perhaps this presiding 'star' radiance helps to explain why there

---

[4] In a minor key, the dominant and subdominant keys will have relative majors—on the seventh and sixth degrees of the scale respectively.

lingers an element in Baroque music that, despite being rooted in its tonal structure, has not yet turned its back entirely on being a king in the land of shades. The sheer, vault-shaking magnificence of a Bach toccata and fugue for organ has not yet laid aside its robe of royal purple. Any adolescent travelling 'daily farther from the east', who has been the humble vehicle for bringing such music into the sense world through the effort-demanding control of his lanky flailing shin bones as they put on their final growth spurt, can testify to this. The lifelong elation resulting from this would suggest that the Greek 'beggar on earth', the Ego, begging for sustenance far away from its true home, has still a further step to take as it travels from *spirit* being to *human* being.

★ ★ ★

This transitional point is where Classical music arrives.[5] The harmony in which its themes are couched (especially in quick movements) is elementary compared with Baroque (often stripped down to three or even two basic chords). Harmonically, the themes themselves seem diffidently apron-string tied to their tonic, for all their otherwise vitality—their virile rhythmic invention and distinctly outlined melodic contour. The composers' reticence regarding the harmonic garb in which their expositionary themes are clad, however, undergoes pendulum swings into explorations of harmony which take the listener beyond the limitations we have seen in Baroque. Mozart had a not infrequent habit of plunging into the development section of his sonata form movements with a sense of relieved vigour, if not, on occasion, daring abandon, by liberating himself from thematic material which had already been presented in the exposition.★ These moments of bit-between-the-teeth tonal exhilaration would no doubt be linked by some commentators to *Sturm und Drang*. Suffice it to say here that we find both Haydn and Mozart, the supreme Classicists, more often than not utterly relishing the exploration of those harmonies which nourish deeper veins in the soul than what can come across at times as almost superficially banal I–V harmonic progressions scantily dressed

---

[5] The generic term 'classical music' is not meant here, but that Classical style of which Mozart is one of the major representatives.

in scraps of subsidiary (sometimes verging on the throw away) conventional thematic material.[6]

On the one hand, the individual character of the Classical themes themselves—whistled, one could well imagine, by Viennese butchers as they clenched their fingers round their sharpened knife blades and tore nonchalantly through their ox carcasses!—carries with its clear identity a corresponding element in the soul; with the respective *recognition* of the theme inducing a constant stimulation of the self-identity of the listener, a kind of musical Ego-drip-feed! This element of cut glass thematic identity could be said to have first entered into music (decisively, however primitive) with the 'fantasy-in-echo' genre of the Dutch,[7] following soon after the country's liberation from imperial Spain.[8] (Seventeenth century Dutch genre painting also objectified for the onlooker, and that meant virtually everyone in the country, constant reminders of self and surroundings: one's own home, its sun-filled interior spaces, the privacy of its brick-walled patios, the canal slopping right outside the front door, one's favourite tippling haunt, the familiar fly-pestered cattle down by the shore at sunset, cloud banks in the ever-changing skyscape, the light caught by the sails of a hundred ships, and so on.) However, the musical phrases following closely on one another's heels in the fantasy-in-echo could hardly be called themes. Certainly not in the Classical sense, where the balance that was embedded in the tonal structure of Baroque now rises to the surface, as it were, and is heard *within* each theme (the rise and fall of the opening bars of *Eine Kleine Nachtmusik* provides a good example), and carried to creative extremities in the sometimes bold, sometimes subtle contrasts between each theme and its predecessor and/or successor. The horse, cantering with glee as it pulls the cart through this ever-present scenic contrast, is to be found as much in the rhythmic detail as in the melodic shape of each theme. Even when Haydn, for example, roguishly uses similar snippets of melodic contour in his themes (often to usher in the second subject group), he makes them distinguishable through their rhythmic definition or some other feature.

---

[6] Stamitz (1745–1801) ploughed the virgin Classical land with this, without which the style of Haydn and Mozart may not have been so fertile.

[7] Sweelinck (1562–1621) has left us with rich examples.

[8] See E. Hutchins, 'William the Silent' in *The Golden Blade* 1977.

Thus, even if the thematic material of the Classicist is content to be clad with the simplest of beggar's cloak harmonies by way of accompaniment, the beggar is at least living by his lyric and rhythmic wits. However, while Classical harmony, bar by bar, seems to take a step backwards into hedonistic simplicity compared with the intricately laced harmony of the Baroque, its *tonal design* takes a very bold and decisive step forwards. In the exposition of his sonata form, the Classicist almost invariably restricts himself to the kind of harmonic palette used by his Baroque forerunners—even whittling the palette down to as much as one third of its original—but this constraint is totally cast aside in the development section where the availability of all 24 keys is eagerly drawn upon (with Beethoven and Schubert, meanwhile, waiting in the wings to see how they can effectively contribute to the Ego-drama). Not that I wish to imply that Mozart's propensity for dramatic modulations is confined to the development sections of his sonata forms. The barnstorming change from four flats to three sharps (the keynotes being only a semitone apart!) occurs in one of his most lyrical adagios in K481, the violin sonata in E flat.

★ ★ ★

It is significant that, though the Intellectual Soul had modernized the tuning of musical instruments (something akin to other features in the Age of Enlightenment where we witness thinking frequently drifting away from nature towards the abstract?) the full *tonal* use of that 'well-tempered' (unnatural) tuning had to bide its time until the sun of Classicism had fully dawned. One can certainly find satisfying development sections in sonata form that do not venture beyond the six-fold key structure that was the bread and butter of Baroque composition. But by far the majority of the Classicist's development sections modulate at some point outside—sometimes well beyond—such confines, very often using the wide spectrum of keys at his or her disposal with *harmonically dramatic effect*.

What does this drama in the tonal design signify? Looked at from the point of view of the ever on-going incarnating Ego of humanity, it signifies greater security of feeling in the earthly environment, and that greater Ego security manifests in the confidence of travelling far from home. This is a clear Consciousness Soul phenomenon, parallel with the Industrial Revolution, which was moving apace precisely at this time. Yet the Ego was cautious not to proceed too fast. That the speed of the first steam locomotive was vociferously opposed—lambasted even—by society as a whole as being the work of the devil, gives us an intimation of how far removed from its spiritual home the diving into 'earthly' (mechanical) laws was felt to be. Ego security necessitated a tangible link with home. What else would the common expression of a 'remote key' be referring to? If the Baroque cluster of six keys per movement is likened to a closely related family, Classicism's potential openness towards all 24 keys per movement will mean *ipso facto* that keys are juxtaposed which are relatives at least 'twice removed'! Indeed, there are occasions when we only discover their distant relationship *after* the composer has thrust the juxtaposition well and truly into the listener's Ego-space in a dramatically unheralded way.

So now, in the realm of music, we have looked at some reflections of the full Greek Intellectual Soul recapitulation: the etheric life in Greek sculpture becomes the rhythmic exuberance of the thematic material of the Classical sonata (and other Classical genres); the Ego-in-etheric confidence of Greek conquest becomes the Classical ability to sally forth with tonal confidence into all corners of the musical zodiac (again, in all Classical structures); the Greek assuredness of balance between spiritual and earthly polarities resurfaces in the overall key structure of *sonata form*—form that was not designated as such until c.1840, that is when Haydn and Mozart had long since put the quills with which they wrote their compositions back into the grooves of their writing cabinets. Indeed, even Beethoven had been dead for 13 years by that time. This means that sonata form was something that lived powerfully, universally,[9] overwhelmingly in Classical con-sciousness, and with the creative exuberance of rapids stampeding through a mountain gorge, but *was not felt to be a formative principle needing to be put into words*, any more, say, than did the fact that human beings alternated with left and right legs when they walked! However, we can no longer sideline the fact that this more persistent delving into the revisited Intellectual Soul did not emanate from Paris, but from Vienna.

---

[9] Bach's sons were certainly not bent on prolonging the Baroque.

From Paris to Vienna

This gives rise to two questions, both sides of the same coin: why Vienna? and, why not continue the process in Paris/France? Steiner, after all, sees the baton of evolution being relayed from Italy to France to England. Why this upstart of a Viennese cat among the evolutionary pigeons?

The answer to the questions would seem to lie largely in the social realm. The stringency of French etiquette, something that revolved around the court, would suggest that the fourth member of the human being, the Ego, was somewhat suppressed, made subservient to court procedures. Not that the heyday of France (in the reign of Louis XIV) did not attract strong Egos—architects, writers, composers, painters, generals, theologians and leaders in all walks of life. They incarnated into the socio-political climate and brought about that very quality of Intellectual Soul recapitulation to which Steiner points. But for Egohood itself to thrive, a further step was needed, not the step which led to the blood-bath of the French Revolution or indeed to the somewhat retrograde step of Napoleon assuming the crown of Emperor, but one which nevertheless permitted the shackles in which the aristocracy held the remainder of the population to be loosened. The Ego of the aristocrat could also be said to have gained, despite the shrinking of his purse and influence. England or Holland, one could argue, might also have offered the right circumstances in some respects, but the former was too deeply entrenched in the cogs and clutches of scientific technology, which in turn engrossed the minds of the capitalists, enabling the Industrial Revolution to gain momentum (and ultimately ricochet back from the West into Europe and the rest of the world) while Holland, though unflinchingly stalwart, was still an up-and-coming nation and therefore in the throes of establishing her overseas and other political connections, her pecking order amongst the nations of the New World.

Such a major change in consciousness needed to emanate from an established source. In Austria there existed an extensive empire—as established as any temporal power, subject to the toppling of heads, can be. However, though in some ways linked with Spain through its blue blood, it was far more cosmopolitan. Even well into the nineteenth century, one could see how the air of freedom under the French regime was stifled and therefore the ranging of Ego-hood curbed. In the 1750s, however, the cosmopolitan atmosphere concentrated centripetally, as it were, into the Austrian capital, combined with its wealth of empire and the resultant soul-space which allowed culture to thrive, provided the conditions needed for both an increase in the independence of the individual Ego and the social circumstances for that individuality-blossoming to pour itself into an advance of culture—particularly in the realm of music.

Haydn's circumstances illustrate the point. The wealth, geniality and liberal-mindedness of Prince Esterhazy★ gave the composer the outer assurety and stability needed, relatively untrammelled by external influence, for his genius essentially to give birth to the new style. In Mozart's case it was the precocity nurtured and instilled through his father Leopold's grand tours with him and his sister in their childhood days that must have been a significant and additional factor in the equation that boosted his self-confidence to be in the vanguard of musicians who stepped beyond the economic security of aristocratic patronage into a freelance situation. Add to this the musical effervescence of the Austrian capital which attracted Italians from the south as well as Slavs from the east and serious, even ponderous, German-like attitudes towards art from the north, and you have the recipe which provided the magnetic force that was sufficient to attract the fiery Beethoven, whose advent in Vienna ensured not only the thorough consolidation of Classicism but also the gentle but persistent germination of the seeds of Romanticism. Add all these together and within the mission-accomplished-Intellectual-Soul-recapitulatory transformation of Baroque into Classicism, the way is swept unhesitantly clear for the Consciousness Soul to take centre stage.

★ ★ ★

The confluence in Vienna of Italian and German streams in particular is central to this issue. Mozart, despite his facility with so many genres, has (for him) a long history of coming to terms with contrapuntalism. His valuing of his connection with the Franciscan Padre Martini was

certainly not the result of any religious leanings, but because Martini
shone out as the contrapuntal star in the musical world of Europe in
the latter part of the eighteenth century. Bologna, where he taught,
still retains its flavour of intellectualism in a country which cham-
pioned the Sentient Soul of the present age. The contrast between the
two streams was seen as a *melodic* emphasis south of the Alps and a
harmonic one in the north. But in the 'gallant' style, at its most deri-
sable, south and north were in danger of giving birth to music that was
ill-prepared for the Consciousness Soul—too hasty and too insub-
stantial a plunge into the 'mood of the third'. It was the saving grace of
Mozart's healthy instinct, it seems to me, that sensed that *his* way of
avoiding becoming lemminged along in the plunge would be the
more secure if he could discover, recruit and then have at his com-
mand the essence of what lived in counterpoint.

His own early stammerings in church music (if that is not too dis-
paraging a way of putting it) were steps on the lengthy road to the C
minor Mass K427. His early exercises in counterpoint, for example,
K85 and K116, were steps on the lengthy road to his mastery of the
technique such as we find in the exquisite violin and viola duos K423
and K424. His early admiration for Michael Haydn's★ ecclesiastical
compositions (fugues and items from the Litany as well as copies of
pieces made when Mozart was 17), proved to be steps on the lengthy
road to his own liberation from church music.[1] There is an obviously
inherent connection between the independence of each 'voice',
whether in the orchestra or in chamber music, and Mozart's life–long
quest for counterpoint. The quest had its fun side, of course. At the age
of 22 in a letter to his father he describes an occasion when he was
given a theme for improvization by a priest: 'I took it on a promenade
[played with it both in the major and minor]; finally the theme again
but backwards. Finally I wondered if I might not use the playful
melody as a theme for a fugue . . . it went as accurately as if Daser [a
tailor they knew in town] had measured it for the purpose. The dean

---

[1] His zest for acquiring competency in the style followed the appointment in
1772 of the new archbishop, who by all accounts liked to get the mass over and
done with, particularly when he was celebrating it himself; and of course it was
the friction between Mozart and his employer that led to the widely known
dismissal, and to his subsequent move from Salzburg to Vienna.

was beside himself'. But apart from the fun—and surely he could not have become a stuffy contrapuntist even if he had tried (except to satirize)—what was the driving force that urged him in this direction?

One real possibility is that, for Mozart, counterpoint was one of the main contributory factors in the maturation of his own style, and also a kind of buffer which prevented a premature Classical dive into the Consciousness Soul, all working in parallel with the development of tonality. In this way, at the same time as extending the *Intellectual Soul* exploration of tonality that it had itself engendered through the 'creation' of the diatonic scale or, if preferred, the advance and ennoblement of the Lydian★ mode, across the entire musical globe, Classicism was grooming the Ego in readiness for its next step. The thus strengthened Ego was prepared to be immersed in *that* realm—*for the first time in evolution* it should be emphasized—which is the unadulterated antithesis of its own spiritual home: the physical world with all its outer attitudes and the inner 'laws' which manifest themselves in ways that are quantitatively measurable. In this light, Classicism can be pictured as the vigil of the Ego before it mounts and rides into the adventures of the fully-launched-at-last Consciousness Soul Age.

We have seen how the Classicist's extension of the six-fold key palette handed on by the Baroque composer was intricately connected with sonata form and how this prevailed, inspired and informed the structure of musical composition for some half a century. We see it in the astonishing creativity that flowed lavishly in sonata, concerto, quartet, overture and in other genres, before the bulk of the Classicists output had cooled down sufficiently for the musicologist to approach it with his ice-tinged analytical consciousness and say: all *that* was sonata form. Small wonder, since its features had not been pinned like tropical butterflies to the cork board of the intellect, that its ebullience maintained the hallmark of brilliance and true originality in the hands of its three giants: the jovial Haydn, Mozart something of a cross between mercurial elusiveness and Orphic inspiration, and the Promethean Beethoven. At this point, the baptismal water on the brow of *Chrysostom* will carry us no further and we shall need to advance to the full immersion of *Johann*.

JOHANN

It is conceivable that such music, if properly understood, could not be heard without the hearer having to go through an active process of metamorphosis within himself as the music developed. John Davy[1]

Hebrew Initiates spoke of the inexpressible name of God, of the God who dwells in man, for the name can be uttered only by the soul for this same soul . . . Hence the emotion of wonder which thrilled through the listeners when the name Jahve was uttered, for Jahve or Jehovah signifies I *or* I AM. *In the name which the soul uses of itself, the God begins to speak within the individual soul.* Rudolf Steiner 22.08.1906

---

[1] John Davy, 'The Evolution of Music' in L. Stebbing, *Music, Its Occult Basis and Healing Value*, 1958, New Knowledge Books, pp. 61–67.

Johann at Play

Sprinkle some iron filings onto a horizontal sheet of paper and then touch the paper from beneath with a magnet and what will happen? As we all know from our school-days, the filings suddenly all swivel so that they lie in the direction of the field of magnetic forces, making it visible, as it were, through the pattern which they form. I am taking my cue from this phenomenon by attempting to make the *Ego*—its field of force, if you like—visible. It is, after all, an everyday experience for the large majority of the population. I do not want to suggest that familiarity always breeds contempt, but we shall need to dive deep beneath the surface of our familiarity with the Ego for our present enquiry. To begin with, I shall not go out of my way to connect one filing to the next. This I shall turn to once I have reasonably saturated the concept of Ego. What we might call Johann 'at play' will at that point transform into a more obviously purposeful application of our knowledge of Ego.

The Ego is that element in our human constitution which singles us out from the other kingdoms of nature: mineral, plant, animal. We have a physical body in common with the mineral world: we suffer from anaemia if the blood lacks iron; we suffer from caries if the teeth lack calcium and so on. Our physical body is imbued with life forces (etheric) in common with the plant world. As plants vary in their degree of vitality, so do we. Some plants are so vigorous that they can be propagated by the most dabbling of gardeners taking cuttings, whereas other plants do not even send out new shoots from the parent plant once a stem has been cut off, irrespective of whether the gardener is an amateur or a professional. We also, like plants, vary in our level of etheric forces. Still considering taking cuttings: in the case of many plants this is best done at certain times of the year when the life-forces are at their strongest.

These two elements in our constitution, physical and etheric, attract (for instance each morning when we wake) our sentient nature (astral organization in Steiner's terms; soul or psyche also indicate a like perception in other cultures). Our sentient nature we have in common with the various animal species, the commonality being expressed in a whole Noah's ark of figures of speech: bull at a gate, stubborn as an ass, rabbiting on about something, watching like a hawk, dog-in-a-manger, a queer fish . . . In addition, the fourth principle is the Ego—that which gives us identity; the self; that which enables each of us to call ourselves a 'free spirit'; entelechy; individuality; that which English speakers designate as I, Germans as *ich*, French as *je*, Italians as *io*, Russians as *ya* (phonetic), Dutch as *ik*, Greeks as *ego* and so on. With *Ego* we are back home again, back to the *self*, hopefully having succeeded in circumnavigating other uses of the word that have flickered on the screen of Western thought. The Ego, on the wings, so to speak, of the sentient (astral) organization ushers in wakefulness, transmits its own nature in self-consciousness. Thus the Ego has a *double existence*: that of which we are conscious when it 'inhabits' our physical- and life-organizations, or 'returns' to those organizations after a period of being asleep or unconscious, and that of which we are largely unaware when we are wrapped in deep sleep or go into a coma. For the moment, we may leave on one side the question of the Ego at and after death.

Our *degree* of self-consciousness varies, too. Not only from day to night. It normally increases during childhood, sometimes at certain nodal points in leaps and bounds. It fluctuates in illness and tiredness—often, in these circumstances, closely connected with our vitality. Even a single limb can 'go to sleep' momentarily and we may experience when in such a state that Ego consciousness does not extend into the limb as it normally does. Language is teeming with phrases and idioms that relate to or describe different conditions of 'self'—what a treasure house of common wisdom it is. It is, perhaps, noteworthy that such expressions predominate in negative Ego situations, suggesting that we generally take the normal waking condition for granted. We *drift off*. We are *all there*. We do not know whether we are *coming or going*. We *lose the plot*. We are *inconsistent*. We *take hold of ourselves*. We are *wrappable round someone's little finger*. We are *not quite focused. Butter wouldn't melt* . . . We are *concentrated*. Or its opposite. We feel *confidence* or *diffidence*. We go on *Ego trips*. When veering towards the inconsiderate we become *egotistical*. We are *fallible*. Simply *not there. Not with it. She's a bright one* (usually referring to someone's child). We are *disorientated*. We are *at sixes and sevens*. We *stargaze*; *day-dream, go wool-gathering, have blind spots, become light-minded, fly-off at a tangent* or we succumb to or enjoy the thousand and one other conditions for which the language can produce very precise and subtle expressions. One of the most illuminating of these, perhaps, is *presence of mind*. Its opposite *absent*-mindedness raises the question of *what* is present one moment and where does that 'what' disappear to when 'absent'? A question we can leave simmering until the meat of it gets a bit more digestible. However, 'presence' of mind and 'absent-mindedness' seem to epitomize what all the other expressions are referring to in their several ways: presence or absence of Ego, to whatever degree, in whatever mood.

None of these terms applies to the other three kingdoms of nature, at least not in a straightforward manner. An absent-minded bison or a slice of confident sandstone are not items we expect to be displayed in a mail-order catalogue or a charity shop window. However, we may transpose terms from one kingdom to the next as metaphors if we wish to describe some particular characteristic—a *shy* violet comes to mind, as does the conspicuous tree known in Spanish speaking countries as the *flamboyant*. The other way round too, where we describe Ego conditions by borrowing from the other kingdoms of nature: like a *rock*; *swanning* around; a dark *horse*; a rough *diamond*; shifting *sand*; good as *gold*; *feather* brained.

With regard to 'inhabiting', a concept that lends itself well to an understanding of the Ego, Steiner described the other three members as its *sheaths*. Could this be why little children are invariably taken at some point in their play with Russian dollies? The Ego inhabits its sheaths. It incarnates, a concept particularly valuable for pedagogical research, in that it is during childhood that the Ego's incarnating into its sheaths is drawn out over a long period—which is one way of characterizing what childhood actually is. This natural time process is best not meddled with if we want healthy children and sane societies, though there may be rare exceptions: Mozart, for one.

If we receive a political campaigning pamphlet, it will probably be addressed to the *occupant*, a purely utilitarian use of the word, one halibut next to the next on the fishmonger's slab. However, the occupant is not only the one whom the 'left or right' stuffer of envelopes hopes to inveigle into voting in a particular way, he or she is also the *home-maker*, the one who not only occupies but *transforms* the house into a home. When the Ego is 'at home' it brings with it into its sheaths qualities from its metaphysical existence. Notwithstanding, because it is a *free spirit* these qualities can be positive or negative, good or bad. This moral or immoral streak in the Ego affects the sheaths which, so to speak, do its bidding. And with the other three kingdoms of nature? There is no question of granite being good or bad in any moral sense. It simply IS. Its degree of suitability for building or road metal is another matter. In some such context, we might apply the concept of good to the mineral world. Michelangelo had an uncanny eye for spotting a good piece of marble in the quarry. On the shadow side, a rogue builder might have an uncanny eye for the gullible customer on whom, when installing a bathroom, he can palm-off a cracked piece of marble! Similarly with the plant world. A wood carver might opt for lime or oak, while the cross-grain quality of elm is not as 'good' for the job. Weeds, as we refer to them, are plants that grow in places where the conditions for their flourishing are good but where humans take a dim view of their presence. Not that things started like that when we were at the proverbial hunting and gathering stage. Hawkweed* (all one word) is a fairly common wild flower. The fact that 'weed' features as a part of the name by which we identify it does not conjure forth the sort of feelings that you might have on seeing groundsel* smothering your prize shallots after you have spent a fortnight's holiday away from home and away from your precious allotment. Weather forecasters are some of the worst culprits. Seldom do they refer to rain, say, as a pure mineral (H_2O) in objective terms. No one takes exception to rainy weather after a drought but why, one wonders, when meteorology is after all a science, speak of wet weather apologetically or conveying varying shades of disapproval?

Still higher up the scale than mineral or plant, we might overhear the huntsman say, 'Good dog', as he gives his mud-bedraggled retriever a friendly pat, but if we leave the chicken house unlocked one night and get away with it, we do not think, 'Good fox!' On the contrary, we put it down to a stroke of luck and reflect, 'That was a near one!' Or if the fox wreaks havoc we ascribe it to instinct (genetic predisposition) or some such, cringe and pensively lick our wounds as we inspect our bank balance before heading off to replenish our stock at the next poultry market. Conversely, we take action if a shoplifter is caught—never mind if we are of the 'genetic predisposition' school of thought or not. We expect the Ego to do something about its inherited genes. Use its talents. Tackle its shortcomings. Even a kleptomaniac can undergo therapy to enable the Ego to take hold of its hands. Let the fang be never so rapacious, or the claw never so bloodstained, '*red* in tooth and claw' is a concept worlds apart from being caught '*red*-handed'. The former world is Ego-less though viciously instinctual—would it be unfair to say, Darwinian? The fanged and clawed world of red blood's physicality. The latter world is that of the human Ego, at least a regrettable aspect of it. A world in which we hope that the red of shame surging also through the blood might bring the Ego to its sense of self-respect. As humans we can be responsible/irresponsible, trustworthy/untrustworthy, reliable/unreliable. Here we are treading linguistically close to dependent/independent which, in turn, is getting very near to the bull's-eye of our Ego target—but more of that in due course.

Freedom and Responsibility

From a certain point of view Darwin was the perfect butt for the
bishop's taunt: 'Now let me see, Darwin, is it on your mother's side or
on your father's that you are descended from the apes?' However, no
bishop's mitre can replace the bishop's Ego, let him wear half a dozen
mitres piled up on top of one another all at once as, in step behind the
chaplain who is bearing his crosier, he solemnly processes along the
aisle, beneath the cathedral's vaults and bosses and flanked by its arcade
of Gothic arches! Forget the ecclesiastical trappings and the sanctuary
door-knocker, it's the Ego that counts, as the twelfth century carver of
the west façade of Chartres well knew when he prominently displayed
a little band of triumphant devils urging wayward nuns towards hell's
mouth. Are devils more sharply alert for the self-righteous? When
once we were accustomed to crowning kings, our fealty towards them
carried with it a degree of uncertainty. As we knelt, we *prayed* for the
monarch. Yet despite the stonemason's admonishing statuary, we did
not pray for the archbishop—or certainly not in the same manner. By
virtue of his office we expected him to be an unfalteringly reliable
'good boy'.

As touched on earlier, Shakespeare plumbed the depths of kingship,
but as with the fairy tale, his image, be it at the Lady Macbeth/Iago★
end of the scale or the Prospero/Paulina★ end, applied to any- and
everyone in the audience. Shakespeare's greatness, however unsurpassable he was as a dramatist, 'literally' head and shoulders above the
rest of us, lay in his ability to leave absolutely no Ego-stone unturned
and anoint what he discovered there (be it the genie-out–of–the-bottle
that whirlwinded the unkempt Lear or the guilt–ridden Alfonso★) in
the art which flows from the chalice of the Logos, in such a way as to
drive the point home to its very psychological foundations in the souls
of an audience comprised of Egos who were on the cusp of entering a
new age of Ego consciousness. Whilst he was quick to uphold mag-
nanimity, compassion, purity, loyalty and suchlike virtues, he was
equally shrewd at spotting a flaw in the Ego's moral marble slab. Since
we are still essentially on or not far from that same cusp we find him

time and time again undated, less so, surprisingly enough, than some later writers who use far fewer archaisms in their language! The laurel wreath of the Ego is the capital 'I' of Immortality.

Tread on the corns of the Ego's free spirit and you will be asking for it. With their post-'victory' heavy casualties causing alarm at home (summer/autumn 2005) and the Pentagon to dither, backing off the notion that war can be waged against a *principle*, the war the United States 'declared' on terrorism is turning towards becoming a national embarrassment. A third millennium tilting at windmills. The grimmest fears would be a hollow echo of Vietnam. In Britain it hurled politicians and lawyers into gridlock. The politician wants to prove his point and treat the suspected terrorist as a prisoner of *war*. The lawyer takes issue with that because of the lack of any internationally recognisable *declaration* of that war or at ground level any worn uniform that shows clearly that the prisoner is an embodiment of the principle (terrorism), let alone in the face of all the conspiracy theories, on which side of the war the suspected person is supposedly fighting, so she puts on her wig and cries: *'civil liberties'*. The military way is to slaughter the body of the enemy, one of the Ego's sheaths (cf. the farmer who simply shoots the fox—not because he is a naughty fox, but simply because part of the farmer's livelihood depends on the sale of eggs). The lawyer's way is to create an unambiguously clear, black and white framework within which Ego and Ego reside in reasonably mutual harmony. But it is not only lawyers. Any legal ambience is composed of three entities: i) that of the law *makers* (which, in an age of terrorism, includes the very uncomfortably fitting politician's 'hat'); ii) those branches of the judiciary which *maintain* the law—judges on high, bobbies on the beat, bouncers on the door, Inland Revenue officers and a gaggle of other bureaucrats on the other end of the automated, button-pressing message you are 'welcomed' by if you try to speak to them on the phone! and iii) your own *conscience*. (It is on my mind.)

★ ★ ★

Conscience!—that attribute of the Ego which combats (with its own Ego-derived power) the enticements, temptations, allurements and seductions of everyday—every night, too—life. Never mind what we call the power that would lure the Ego away from the straight and narrow, from 'genetic predisposition' to ... we-are-only-human-after-all to ... 'Beelzebub'! The lure is a given, an inescapable quotidian phenomenon. The results vary, of course. And accountability is meted out according to society's perception of the Ego involved. A hangover after a bout of binge drinking is manifestly our own silly fault. Whether we get sympathy or condemnation, it is a private affair. But step over the boundary of the law and all our peccadilloes' privacy evaporates in the public mesh of legal proceedings. Society accepts *minors per se* as humans still requiring support in the domain of their Ego activity; but it keeps other Egos off the streets, if they fail beyond a certain point in self-control by using asylums, international extradition treaties and deportment protocols, on the spot fines, Her Majesty's prisons, driving licence endorsements and a dozen and one other official devices in its dubious attempt to stem the tide of legal effrontery. ('Dubious', that is, if radical, pre-emptory steps are not first taken in the field of education.)

Severity, legal rigour, lies at the centre of this mesh, but at the fringe the Ego's potential weaknesses are anticipated where necessary and sometimes when unnecessary, alas, often when we find ourselves thrown into the same legal boat as the one in which a felon has been rowed away to his island of solitary confinement. The motorist (whose Ego has sometimes been described as acquiring a kind of fourth sheath: his car!) has to contend with a barrage of *thou should nots*: parking metres, traffic wardens, speed restrictions, speed cameras, supposedly inhibiting yet what looks like a losing battle tax on petrol, tolls ... all to 'save' his Ego from consciously exercising common sense, courtesy, social conscience and care for the environment. The university undergraduate has to contend with assignment deadlines, stringent exams, escalating library-book fines, academic disciplines of one kind and another, even the threat of being 'sent down', etc., to 'save' his Ego from having to choose to work in an honourable way, and to save his tutors' Egos from having to exercise discernment and free judgement about his talent, his ability to apply himself, his scholarly integrity and the standard of his work, as they sit in one meeting after another or sweat away after the end of term filling in forms that are required by the Senate. The failings of one generation become the once-bitten-twice-shy, legally enforced encroachments on the freedom of the Egos of the next generation. The breakdown of trust deteriorates into petty rules and regulations at a domestic or parochial level, or, at a national level, into a horrendously time-consuming, initiative-destroying, self-respect-demeaning flood of legislation, with man-hours (potentially *creative* man-hours) engulfed in *paperwork*, a euphemism for one of the greatest attritions of human dignity and freedom of modern times. Anyone who travelled within the Soviet bloc before the Berlin Wall came down will have experienced some of the extremities of an Ego-denying social order. A far cry from the days when the Ygdrasil tree of Norse mythology stood unshakeably strong in the human psyche, a time long before the fjord-skirting Norwegian spruces harboured any fear of paper-mills.

Fortunately, although I have laboured the point, it is not the only side of the story. We do not all land up in clink. And some of us do precisely *because* the Ego, bursting at the seams of injustice, blazes a trail of civil disobedience. Long live Gandhi, Rosa Parks and co! The story of the Ego is not simply black and white.

The use of the word 'explicable' by a politician at the beginning of the English parliament's 2005 summer recess when the latest suicide bombing incidents in London were being discussed, produced a media furore, resulting in an unprecedented number of broadcasting hours being commandeered as high profile interviewers and interviewees tooth-picked their way through the champing dentures of party rivalry and were displayed in the stocks of political opportunism, stirred up by deliberate or undeliberate flouting of the most elementary, nursery slope logic—all at the expense of the murderers. No one seemed the slightest bit interested in how an Ego could end up becoming a suicide bomber. *Suicide!* Most reactions were of unmitigated (even if diplomatically expressed) outrage at the thought that an Ego should *care* (which is presumably what the user of the e-word did), at least a bit, about another Ego's end-of-the-road state of mind enough to suggest: It *is* explicable! Suicide bombing may be incomprehensible, profoundly unjustifiable, inexpressibly tragic, in no way excusable, anathematizable as far as any religious creed is concerned, not even politically condonable from a so-called Christian, so-called democratic, so-called Western view point. But unless a true, sober, unprejudiced explanation is found, global society will surely never be able to *begin* to solve the problem that the Ego-tragedy of it presents. A nun who has taken the veil may have gone an Ego journey that is equally incomprehensible to many—especially if she has confounded the twelfth century devils. But wherever people's meandering destinies take them, it behoves us, surely, to respect the other Ego, at least to the extent of *understanding*. The physical and etheric sheaths of the human being are, in the main, and in many respects, predictable—certainly by comparison with the unpredictability of the Ego and its astral sheath. But given perseverance, time and insight, they too, and the puzzling destiny deriving from them, must surely be *explicable*.

The Connection with Music

We saw in an earlier section what a vital part the human Ego had to play in the *development* of consciousness: its immersion in the etheric organization that gave rise to the Intellectual Soul in Ancient Greece (and in the onward tread of time through Ancient Rome and the Middle Ages); its furthering of the Sentient Soul in modern European times initially through the tidal wave of Renaissance culture; its furthering of the Intellectual Soul in still more recent times, initially through the ascendancy of French culture and so on. Those Soul qualities (I retain the initial capital to emphasize the proper noun status of what we are concerned with) are reflected in all aspects of culture, and the pursuit of what in musical style led us to Mozart. Indeed when Edward Dent remarked (in the first chapter of his *Mozart's Operas*) that 'our appreciation of [Mozart] today is in many cases quite consciously a scientific appreciation',[1] he expressly states that that *scientific appreciation* was the result of musical education having advanced. We could all agree that science has advanced since then—Dent was writing in the '40s of the last century—though we might want to debate the ethics of that advance here and there. Music education, on the other hand, the excellence of Chetham's School of Music in Manchester and the like notwithstanding, has, if anything, been drastically marginalized at school level. Scientific appreciation obviously accords with the flourishing of critical analysis at academic level, at least the scientific half of it. But what it is that does the 'appreciating' in our human make-up is something that has remained either unaddressed or, at most, implicit. Focusing on the human Ego from a spiritual scientific point of view does, I believe, begin to make that appreciation through understanding more explicit. In doing so we are moving the *quite* of Dent's 'quite consciously' into a *more* mode—a still more conscious understanding—which Mozart's ambrosial talent surely deserves.

★ ★ ★

---

[1] E. J. Dent, *Mozart's Operas*, 1947, OUP.

In order to sharpen the focus on the lengthy road of our enquiry a second concept introduced by Steiner will be of inestimable value. In that it refers once more to the several members in our whole human constitution, it is linked to the first concept (the part the Ego has to play in evolution). Here, Steiner approaches the matter by researching how our various members are related to the arts.[2] In brief, we perceive music with the soul, albeit via the ear for most of the time, but not exclusively so: music is accessible to many who can 'read' a musical score just as poetry is accessible when we read it on the printed page, if not as tellingly as when we hear it well recited. Equally, the soul can 'perceive' the music through memory, possibly more effectively than the memory perception of something the eye has once seen, though I am not bent on arguing this point since I am probably biased. Perceiving music with the soul is sufficiently generalized a concept for people to be able to identify with. However, *in* the act of music perception it is not soul substance *per se* that comes across, and this perhaps extends the point of being scientifically appreciative to being *spiritually-scientifically appreciative*. According to Steiner, what is expressed in music are the *laws of the Ego*.[3] When the soul perceives music, the experience is moved by, nurtured by, consoled, inspired, energized, call it what you will, by virtue of the fact that *music is infused with the laws of the Ego*.

To interrogate this we need to go further than merely looking at what Ego means to a modern person: the Johann at play we met earlier in this section will need to advance. It may therefore help to take a side glance at the word's origin: the way the Greek expressed the experience of 'I'. We will then need to extract what the laws governing the Ego might be and then, as a further step, look for their equivalence in music—with a particularly discerning eye on Classical style and an extra discerning eye on the non-ephemeral Mozart.

Since the idea of successive earth lives was self-evident for Greeks who identified with Plato's image in *The Republic*—souls between the planetary spheres and the earth, rising and descending—we may

---

[2] See R. Steiner, 1935 'The Bearing of Spiritual Science on Art' in *Art as seen in the Light of Mystery Wisdom*, Rudolf Steiner Press, 1996, pp.15–33.
[3] Ibid.

imagine the three essential stages in this, bearing in mind that, while for the Egyptian (see *The Book of the Dead*) the journey after death was of paramount importance, life for the Greek was a matter of celebrating being incarnated on the earthly plane. *Better a beggar on earth than a king in the Land of Shades.*

Thus, immersing our imagination in the three Greek sounds: ε γ ω yet consciously risking expressing the imaginative findings in pedantic terms:

E (ε)—the entelechy entertains the idea of the descent to earth,
    at the high point of its journey through spirit land since its previous earth life;
    and full of spirit wisdom it prepares to embody a new physical frame
    by retracing its earthward bound steps through the planetary spheres.

G (γ)—the entelechy gropes its way into the embryonic stage of development;
    rejoicing in the gifts with which the planets have endowed it;
    yet gradually gainsaying the spiritual support of the hierarchies;
    while grasping outer earthly conditions,
    guarding against too strong an influence from those powers that would lead it astray;
    and thence goes the way of its karma.

O (ω)—the entelechy having to open itself to what it receives from its inherited genealogy,
    'obeys' its higher decision in meeting its karma;
    orders its new life;
    occupies itself with what comes towards it;
    and orphans itself from the spirit
    so that it becomes endowed with the requisite freedom
    to act in such a way that orientates as positively and as humanly possible towards future lives.

Though the Greek may have *used* the hours in the day differently from the way we do, the shadow of his sundial told the same temporal story as ours. Similarly, if we subscribe to the concept of the Ego reincarnating, the time scale has to take the metaphysicality of the Ego's other home seriously into account. At night we are more than absent-minded. We *go out like a light*. *Out of the body* is a common enough concept, but it is too general to answer the question: out where?

John Field (1782–1837) was an early Romantic composer. His nocturnes for the then new-fangled pianoforte are still played. The idea of a composer writing a piece entitled 'nocturne' is intriguing. The Romantics bemoaned in their several ways the passing of a former age. Put simplistically, industrialism they saw as usurping the world in which humans were humane, nature was natural, and divinity was divine. They saw the slope of evolution sliding ignominiously towards an inhumane, unnatural and unatheistic abyss. The question was, therefore, how to wrench human consciousness from the thrall of technology, how to de-mechanize the soul, and ultimately, how to reinstate the spirit? They cantered off in various directions chasing after vanishing ideals, fast-fading imagination, neglected Gothic, forgotten nature and so on. Field (and, of course, Chopin★) turning to one of these directions, awoke to the significance of sleep—that is, through the mood in their nocturnes they sought to draw attention to the importance of what happens to consciousness during the hours of sleep. Somewhere there, they must have felt (mustn't they?) that sleep offered an entrée into the problem of the lost consciousness of a spiritual existence. Such feelings were undoubtedly Ego driven. The machine was driven by physical laws. Unduly long factory hours fettered human life to the individuality-defacing, soul-destroying, tick of the 24-hour-a-day clock. Incarnations, on the other hand, are to do with *cosmic* time; an Ego dimension where a day in any given earthly life has to be seen in conjunction with those Cosmic days which signify the duration of successive lives. This, in terms that Steiner explained, is connected (even mathematically) with the *Precession of the Equinoxes*. If sleep is the 'little death', earthly life, with its many sleeps, can be seen as the mirror of cosmic life with its many incarnations.

The Ego, in returning to inhabit a new body in its next earthly life, then has the opportunity, a) to experience and assimilate where evolution has got to during the intervening time, for example, what other Egos have meanwhile accomplished, b) to advance the mind (Shaw's actress's dalliance with the notion of 'brains' was surely at least a token whimper of acknowledgement that the mind's ascendancy was part of the divine plan),[4] c) to make some contribution to evolution (though the quantum, quality and value of contributions vary enormously from Moses to the unknown Israelite, from Mrs Pankhurst to the unknown washerwoman, from Alexander the Great to the unknown soldier), and d) to offer some restitution for past deeds of discordance perpetrated by the Ego (for example, Moses was not allowed to accompany the Children of Israel across the Jordan to enter the Promised Land). And that 'adjustment' for imperfection was within one life. How about the unsung deeds of the soldier, known or unknown, major or minor, exemplary or reprehensible, saintly or damnable? In a new life the melody of those unsung deeds blossoms again in the roses and (equally necessary) the thorns of destiny. But from a karmic viewpoint the Ego is still free—free to perform deeds of restitution *or not*. Free to go further and perform deeds of self-sacrifice *or not*.

A cheque sent off for the relief of famine in a drought-riven area of West Africa is the sort of off-the-cuff example of self-sacrifice we run into every day. But one can think of plenty of instances where self-sacrifice endures the best part of a lifetime—not only in the lives of philanthropists or canonized saints. There are areas of fascinating shades of grey too. I was once being driven by a friend to Mexico City airport, from the town where I had been lecturing on 'the Development of Human Consciousness as Reflected in Music', when we passed a bunch of stationary vehicles—crumpled metal and shattered glass scattered at the roadside and drivers, decidedly unstationary, gesticulating animatedly amidst the rubble. To a foreigner, the scene looked aggressive and certainly heated, but I learnt that the hullabaloo was not, in fact, taking place out of a motivation of personal animosity. Where an accident occurs (not infrequent if abandoned wrecks and reckless driving were anything to go by), my friend informed me,

---

[4] A reference to the proposal Bernard Shaw received from the ravishing vision in sunglasses who was moved to have a child by him on the grounds of what a wonderful union *his brains and her looks* would make. And Shaw's boorishly chauvinistic retort which he somehow got away with: 'Madam, have you considered the eventuality that our progeny would be hampered with if it inherited *my* looks and *your* brains?'

everyone who can gets out of their vehicle and enquires who has insurance. Hopefully one person in the pile-up will have. Then comes the relieved and unanimous: 'Right, it's *your* accident!' Corrupt? To the Western mind whose Ego is so frequently saved the responsibility of taking initiative—yes. Not that I am advocating that initiative is applicable quite in this way, of course! But to the dollar-under-dog in the Developing World, who is somewhere in between what was once an Ego-prompted free deed in such circumstances and what is now perceived to be an insurance racket, such a procedure would appear to be a neighbourly solution to a way of exploiting the current fashion of being 'economical with the truth'.

At first sight this hardly looks like self-sacrifice. It would be easy to dismiss it superciliously as an example of the corruption known or suspected to have riddled the country from the Head of State down. Legally, undoubtedly there is something awry. But from the point of view of the Egos who are forcibly brought together in adverse circumstances and who mutually find a way . . . ?? It is worth thinking over. Might there not even be a homeopathic trace of the Ego transforming evil into some resemblance of good? A desperate response to the inadequacy of a system in which the power-hungry predators at the top of the pile nonchalantly leave the have-nots to stew in unadulterated squalor and/or to the tender mercies of the 'heads' of an organized religion which mercilessly inquisitioned lingering ancient Mayan civilization and the social order of its Aztec successors, pleading, no doubt, that they were merely the ministers of some imperative bout of divine sabre-rattling.

We now need to withdraw the microscope from the exercise of peering at each iron filing and discern the pattern all the filings are making together, that is, to determine from all the Ego phenomena at hand what might reveal the fingerprints of the *laws of the Ego* and therefore be enlisted for our onward journey to a deeper understanding of Mozart.

Laws of the Ego

It is almost unthinkable that all the composers in Classical style should never have conceptualized that most Classical of all musical structures: *sonata form*. Nevertheless, the final conceptualization of it according to *The New Grove* appears to have been in 1840. That resonates if distantly with the process of baptism—a naming ceremony which is much more than a tag tied to the baby's wrist in the maternity ward. After the lunar months of gestation in which all the astounding developments which occur when a new human body is being created take place, and, at full term, after the birth and the first assimilation of nourishment through the mouth and digestive system and of air through the lungs, after all that, the *name* is given: Wolfgang Amadeus or whatever.

In the case of identifying sonata form as such, we have hundreds upon hundreds of examples all in all, solely from the Classical period. There is therefore perhaps something more typical about the process than naming a single individual. Just as the Book of Genesis puts the words, 'Let us make Man in our own Image' into the mouths of the Elohim[1] so something in the human psyche must have been saying to composers: Let us compose in sonata form, *but at the same time, let us remain utterly flexible in interpreting the law which presides over this form, thus enabling the greatest compositions to take place before anyone has the chance of spoil-sporting our play by throwing a spanner into our creative workshop!* Presumably it was not until the process had run its astonishingly productive course with hosts of symphonies, sonatas, string quartets and other chamber works, etc., resounding through the Orphic corridors of heaven, that someone with a musicological turn of mind came along and, following the mighty Elohim proclamation, 'who saw that it was good' (exceptionally good some would add) squeaked the words: *It* is sonata form.

Steiner's references to the Ego are not quite as myriad as the stars, yet they stud the 'azure vault' of his shared research in a similar way. So on

---

[1] See Hebrew word for God in Genesis 1.

the one hand we have a seemingly coming down with a conceptual bump from the star-endowed heights of inspiration with his: *music conveys the laws of the Ego*, while, on the other hand, the concept is an immense stimulation to creative enquiry. In addition, therefore, to having joined in the 'Johann at play' I shall now lean back to observe what constellation patterns emerge from Steiner's myriad of references, leaving it to readers to determine for themselves whether each constellation can be classified as a one-star, two-star, three-star, four-star or five-star Ego *law*.

[1] The Ego came into being as a *spiritual entity* and therefore either on the surface or deep down feels spirit realms to be its true home. Yet it is also at home on earth, indeed, *needs* earth for its stages of development.

[2] The *earthly (physical)* body it inherits is sustained by an etheric organization and made sentient by an astral organization—the Ego's three sheaths. Incarnating into its three sheaths enables the Ego to be *aware of itself.* When leaving the earthly body (in sleep, for example) the Ego and astral mostly have to forego that awareness.

[3] The two Ego habitations are thus a polarity, symbolized in the age-old contrast of heaven and earth, which, if they are considered side by side, in many respects constitute an *incongruency*.

[4] This incongruency is the basis for the Ego's sense of *humour* even to the extent of laughing (Chaucer-wise) at itself in response to the Ego—snared, perhaps, in the extremes of feigned piety or downright profligacy. The quaintness of the frog (an unthreatening amphibian) in the fairy story 'Iron Hans'* could be regarded as a child-friendly example of this.

[5] The Ego thus reflects in its own nature the nature of the two worlds: *the outer, sense perceptible world* and *the world of spirit*.

[6] During the Ego's earthly life, the comparative remoteness of the world of spirit means that it is associated with an *air of mystery* and for some, disbelief, an attitude of mind that has prevailed over some centuries now, since positivistic consciousness (like birds over Nagasaki on that fateful day in August 1945)

scorched the feathers from the wings of human thought so that it fell lifeless into matter.

[7] Notwithstanding, the Ego has *access to both* exoteric (sense perceptible) and esoteric (supersensible) realms.

[8] The Ego *enters into its earthly life* in order to be part of evolutionary progress both actively and passively.

[9] After 25,920 days of earthly life (to take a figure as an average which has astronomical-cosmic associations, rather than the more customary threescore years and ten) the Ego *returns to its spiritual home*. Neither figure is, of course, to be taken as an absolute.

[10] The process of earthly death and new birth is *repeated* (not uncommonly, twice in 2160 years) so that the Ego can continue its progress when *new cultural conditions* prevail on earth, conditions conducive to its own evolution. The true Ego as an eternal entity, never wilts. Human despair signifies losing touch with the Ego.

[11] The Ego *learns* through these experiences of earthly life and through *responding* to them.

[12] Because of the *free spirit* that the Ego feels itself rightfully to be, it is also approachable by non-progressive powers who influence it to bring about immoral deeds in one degree or another. Milton monumentally describes *human discord* with the words: 'disproportioned sin/Jarred against nature's chime, and with harsh din/Broke the fair music that all creatures made . . .' in his *At a Solemn Music*. His is the large canvas vision of our going astray but we all know the sticky-postage-stamp version of it. And in our darkest moments we can feel overpoweringly assailed by the opposing powers. Something of that quality is expressed in the slow movement of the Piano Sonata in A minor K310 (bars 37–50) where the music seems in the throes of indeterminacy and is pushed to near despair (see Appendix B).

[13] All the same, in the long run, what appear on the surface to be retrogressive deeds provide a further opportunity for progress through the Ego being given the freedom to *resolve the discordance* they have created—the process of *karma*. Karma as distinct from determinism.

[14] That same quality of freedom gives rise to another Ego man-
      nerism: *unpredictability*; but this is not in conflict with the Ego's
      strong connection with the predictability attached to whatever
      laws obtain in other domains where freedom is *not* an attribute.

[15] Through resistance to the non-progressive powers the Ego
      gains autonomous strength—*self-confidence*. In its calmest form
      this could perhaps best be described as being self-possessed.

[16] The Ego's self-confidence a) expresses itself in *self-assertion*; but
      b) is subject to going too far and becoming *egotistical*.

[17] The Ego has the task of finding the *balance* between too much
      or too little expression of itself on its long road to achieving an
      egotistically free self-assertion.

[18] As the Ego a) gains in self-knowledge, so b) it can summon up
      greater and greater powers of *endurance*.

[19] During this process of Ego evolution it can extend and project
      its own habitancy of two worlds by a) *bringing spirit into matter*
      and b) *raising matter towards spirit*.

[20] This implies and necessitates that the Ego is endowed with
      transformative powers.

[21] Not only endurance, self-assurance, humour etc., the Ego can
      exercise the power of *self-sacrifice*, compassionately foregoing
      some benefit that could accrue to itself perhaps, for the sake of
      others or for the earth's well-being or for evolution as a whole.

[22] In order to do this, the Ego has concomitantly to develop the
      power of *discernment* (selflessly identifying the other's need) and
      tact (in offering/giving what it has to offer/give).

The reader's acquaintance with the Ego—something which is both
guaranteed, and which could not be more personal—and which I trust
the foregoing has prodded into increased awareness, will no doubt lead
to an awareness of other Ego qualities and the 'laws' from which those
qualities emanate. The above 'list' is not designed to be comprehen-
sive. At the same time, in its all-roundness it provides a reasonably
sufficient basis for exploring the music under our consideration:
enough to make the exploration not too general, thereby producing
results that are neither hasty and unconvincing, nor so detailed that the
process becomes pernickety and psychologically grilling.

The First Movement of Mozart's
Piano Sonata K533

The next stage, in which the foregoing considerations culminate, smacks unavoidably of formal musical analysis. Consequently, before starting the process I will state my worst fear and at the same time my highest aspiration. How can we analyse so that the *head/intellect* though fully engaged does not remove us further and further from the music, but so that through awakening to the intricacy and wonder of all that the composer's art and 'craft' has implanted in the sound phenomena that waft towards us, we are not thrust into our heads but brought, so to speak, to our knees? With this in mind, while looking at how the laws of the Ego are actually expressed in purely musical, non-verbal terms, I shall proceed to interrogate one of Mozart's most mature works, the Piano Sonata in F Major K533 (1st movement), in such a way that it may awaken an appreciation of his style *from this Ego perspective*. To achieve this, and compensate for the involvement of the intellect that the exercise will entail, I shall frequently use language that I would emphatically eschew in 'formal' analysis.[1] For clarity's sake, I shall refer to the music itself in two ways: bar numbers in Arabic numerals (for example, 223–27), musical motifs in lower case Roman numerals (i, ii, etc.), and to the Ego principle which percolates through Mozart's treatment of the notes, in square brackets [1, 8a, etc.].

The movement (see Appendix C) divides into three 'standard' sections: exposition (1–102), development (102–145) and recapitulation (145–240). We may divide it further: the exposition has a first subject group (1–31), a transition (31–41) and a second subject group (41–102). But as we are not travelling along intellectual highways, but on foot, which is how we need to explore the laws of the Ego, we will

---

[1] This is on the assumption that those readers who do not classify themselves as particularly musical have followed me thus far and are looking forward to continue, even if the ground starts to look rough. (There is, of course, always the beckoning view from the top....)

need the musical equivalent of the kind of details of the journey found
on an Ordnance Survey 1″ map.

The opening half of the first subject—the four bars (1–4)—in which
Mozart has worked three motifs (i) (ii) (iii), steals into the listener's
awareness as if from other worlds [1].

Even though there are plenty of works which arrest the listener's
attention from the beginning (the trombones in the Overture to
The Magic Flute, for example) the anticipatory silence that descends
on an audience just before a piece of music is about to be performed has not only the outer quality of extraneous sounds being
eliminated (not just the pestiferous cellphone) so that the music
alone fills the air as it streams from the future, but also something of
an invitation to the Ego to revisit its *initial* home. A door opener as
well as a curtain raiser.

This phrase (1–4) already contains the principle of repetition [10]
albeit on the smallest of scales (bar 1 and bar 3), though on the second
hearing the longer preparatory note (cf. the crochet C that begins the
piece and the minim C in bar 2) ensures increased Ego awareness [2].

Not only Ego awareness plays in here, however: the descending,
stepwise sequence of notes,

proves to be a motif to which Mozart apportions an archetypal status
and from which, as we shall see, he derives, through transformation,
several of his themes still to come [20]. At the last note of the phrase (4)
the left hand enters (iv) with an accompaniment figure of the most
modest kind [21]

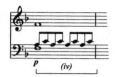

which nevertheless grounds the hovering opening phrase [19a], enabling the continuation (v) of it (5-8), with its chromaticisms (5) and accented passing notes★ (6), to sparkle all the more and lift the humdrum tonic-dominant harmonic swing away from its rootedness in the tonic pedal★ [19b].

Apart from the pure diatonic quality of the first phrase (1–4) and the introduction of chromaticisms into the second phrase (5) as we have noted, Mozart has incorporated further complementary measures into this opening theme [17] in that, a) the first motif (i) is falling and the second (v) rising; b) the first motif (i) begins on the last crochet of the bar, i.e. having an *anacrusis*, while the second motif (v) leads off on the first crochet, the accented beat; and c) the first motif (i) is followed by an inwardly stirring octave leap (2)

while its repetition (3) concludes on a calming whole semibreve (4).

At bar 9 with its upbeat there is further repetition (9–12 repeat 1–4) but with the exchange of the roles of right hand and left hand—spirituality below, as it were, and earthly rootedness above [7] with if anything the tonic anchor (12) being hoisted still higher by the accompaniment figure in the right hand emphasizing the fifth degree of the scale, C, more prominently than the third, A, which was what we heard in the left hand at bar 4. (The mood of the fifth, it will be recalled, lifts present day consciousness outward, while that of the third turns the soul in towards itself.)

The inversion of right and left hands (12–15) a) serves to enhance the Ego's feeling of its two habitations [3], and b) is a profoundly symptomatic stylistic trait of Mozart's which, though profound in meaning, is almost as common as the idiosyncratic blobs of white that spangle a Constable landscape: this is the way that he is wont to shift from one octave to another. One of Mozart's proclaimed ideals was to find the *mean* [17]. He certainly pursues this with all the means at the Classicist's disposal but also frequently does so by taking the listener into the *polarity of upper and lower octaves* and in so doing reflects how the Ego is constantly pulled towards extremes in being exposed to the powers of opposition [12]. Mozart usually does this in such a way that the Ego is left free to orientate, find and affirm itself in between the two octaves [15]. The confidence thus gained here [11] bursts into the new motif at bar 16 (vii).

Within this motif (vii) the Ego's self-awareness is enhanced [16a] through the thrusts provided by the impetuous quavers which accentuate the second and fourth beats of each bar (16 and 17) being soberly balanced [17] at bar 18 by the tied★ note in the right hand depriving even the first beat of the bar of any accent [16b]. The equilibrium thus gained is emphasized still further by Mozart's dynamics which move from *forte* (16) to *piano* (18) and by the cessation of the impelling quaver movement (at 18).

Next we hear a subtle transformation [20] of the four descending quavers of the first motif (i) as Mozart begins to ease the key away from the tonic, F major, to its sharper dominant, C major, by raising the fourth note of the scale, B flat to B natural (bar 22 and intermittently until the piece arrives fully in the dominant key at bar 41). This tonal journey in musical composition is already one that the Ego underwent in Baroque style (typically in *binary*★ movements). There, by the very nature of the Baroque, it tended to drift from one key to the next. Here, it passes clear milestones in the form of intervening keys—D minor (32–33) and C minor (36–37). The greater assurety of the Ego implied by these strongly inserted key contrasts is evidence of the advance that has taken place in the Ego's perception of itself from Baroque to Classical times [15]. Still more of this will surface in the development section of the movement (103–145).

When the device of inverting the parts, right hand and left hand, is taken up again by Mozart (15–19 and 23–27), the diminished★ fifth (19) in the left hand becomes an augmented★ fourth in the right hand in the process (27), and the sounding major seventh of B flat-A in bar 19, second beat, becomes struck major sevenths and a minor second in bars 28–30, the harshest of discords—virtually unprepared—as the motif is extended towards new thematic material in bar 31. The discords, moreover, are highlighted by the *fp* dynamic indication and are rapidly resolved after one quaver, the A passing to G—barely more than Mozartean lip-service to technicalities—but resolved in a more all-embracing way [13] through the fact that essentially all three bars (28–30) consist of only one chord, that of the tonic F major, despite the fleeting canon★ between right and left hands that Mozart embroiders into the counterpoint.

Mozart then demonstrates how quickly, thoroughly and convincingly he can compose a transition, a central feature of the exposition in sonata form, which he does in a matter of 11 wand-waving bars (31–41), actually by following a normal Classical procedure in traditional key change [14], and simply introducing the accidentals★ necessary for the purpose. He thus swiftly moves from the tonic, F major, first to its relative minor, D minor (31–32);

and then through a downward shifting sequence into C major; (33–35) at which point, with an air of mystery [6] he slips, almost imperceptibly (since the flattened third, E flat, is well concealed in the left-hand polyphony to begin with), into the minor (C minor in bar

36), using the minor version of motif (i) repeated instantly four times, over a remarkably arresting harmonic progression in bars 37–38 including the use of the chord of the German sixth (40), with wide upward leaps in the right hand, eventually holding us spellbound through a sudden *piano* to land on a half-close cadence (40).

The delicious ambiguity of whether the Ego has been 'transposed' from the tonic to the dominant via a storm in a teacup or by a dose of Alice in Wonderland is dispelled by the welcoming arms of the so-called second subject group. This begins in conformity with Classical tradition in the dominant key, C major, with a theme scintillatingly diatonic but in its apparent *naïveté* veiling Mozart's equally scintillating and creative mastery of composition [7]. Apart from the left-hand accompaniment figure (43–44) (another example of the Ego's modesty, a role frequently allotted to the left hand and which we found already in bars 4–8 [21]) the theme consists of three motifs: the single *sfz*★ note (41) with which it announces its arrival (ix) and which for an instant obliterates all outer movement while it holds us in suspense; secondly the gently penguin-playing triplets★ (42) that follow (x); and thirdly the rising trills (xi) that conclude the theme in bars 43 and 44.

First let us look more closely at the Ego implications of this passage by considering aspects of balance [17]. The theme we are concerned with (41–45) introduces the second part of the exposition (a large 'half' in this movement cf. 1–41 and 41–102). The balance of the tonic key with its dominant over the period of time involved creates an appetite for further Ego experience in tonality exploration [11] though this is postponed until the development section and so on. Plainer for the eye to see is the balance in the general melodic contour of the descending motif (x) in bar 42 and its rising counterpart (xi) in bars 43–44. The balance of the threshold-crossing chromaticisms in bars 37–42 is followed by the playfully diatonic [4] nature of this theme opening the second subject group, which despite its playfulness is tethered firmly to the dominant key, C major, with no chromaticisms of any kind, not even any accented passing notes worth mentioning.

However, Mozart relieves the theme's well anchored tonality in three ways. Firstly, as the gambolling triplets (x) descend to the new keynote, C, the left hand enters with the triad of C, *not* in its root position but pedestalled on a first inversion, so that during the first beat of bar 43 we hear not CEG but EGC.[2]

The second light touch that Mozart gives is also in the harmony, at bar 45, at the point where the theme concludes, but concludes with an imperfect cadence★ (cf. the perfect cadence★ with which the first theme of the movement concluded at bar 8), a slightly puzzled cock of the eyebrow which is a sure sign of unfinished business.

There are perfect cadences to come (48–49 and 56–57) which give stability, immediately prior to the further working out of the second subject which we shall consider presently. The third light relief is that Mozart enlivens this rather unmitigated diatonic flood-plane through introducing a trickling cascade of trills into motif (xi). Though actually not in this movement, but frequently at the end of a movement or section of a movement, we find a trill on the leading note or as part of the dominant seventh which seems to be the final trump card the composer has to play to enable the Ego to rise through sheer vibrant sound into an exalted inner experience [19b].

Having considered balance, but before moving on, let us now

---

[2] A triad has three positions: root, first inversion and second inversion; in this case E is in the bass.

consider this whole theme (41–45) from the point of view of transformation [20]. Motifs (ix) and (x) essentially describe the five notes of
the descending scale: G F E D C. If we include the upbeat to bar 1, this is
the same melodic contour that we heard at the very beginning of the
movement. Here (41–43), as we have seen, the descending phrase is
colourfully decorated with the triplet figuration. And then immediately
topsy-turvied: for it *ascends* in seven steps B C D E F G A (43–44) or
rather in a sequence of *pirouettes* if we take the trilling into account—a
feature that we shall hear later (66–67) boldly divested of all hyperbole.
Might this contain an element of that which awaits resolution as the Ego
descends with fortitude to earth again [13], once the resolution is behind
it, being experienced as a weight off the Ego's mind?

Though still less than half way through the exposition, Mozart now
begins a lengthy passage in which certain motifs are developed (49–66).
To develop a theme to such a seemingly indulgent and care-free extent
in the expositional part of sonata form is a tribute to the form's
astonishing versatility. Even before Beethoven burst the banks of sonata
form, in Mozart's hands those banks were already flexible, indeed,
ready to spill over into silver-silted deltas of impromptu ebb and flow.
There is already an inkling that this will happen in that motifs (ix) (x)
and (xi) with its trills now transformed into triplets, are virtually
repeated in rising sequence, revisiting *en passant* that key of D minor we
caught a fleeting glimpse of in bars 32–33 (cf. 41–45 and 54–59). To
put icing on this already rich cake, Mozart persistently leads into motif
(ix) with the rising interval (or a variant of it) that we heard in motif (iii).

The musical device Mozart at first uses is *canonic* (49–53), the left
hand inaugurating the canon, not merely with the plain initial motif of
(ix) as we have seen, with the rising interval first heard as motif (iii)—
there it was an octave, here it is variously modified as a fifth, an octave,
a ninth, and another octave. Now an echo★ device in music induces a
quality of Ego awareness [18a]. Imitation★ between parts—into which
the music is about to leap with Cossack-like vigour (57–63)—lies in
the same vein. Strongest of all, perhaps, is what we have here: the
canon. In a canon, already, *while* the experience is happening, despite
the heat of the melodic moment, the Ego is made doubly conscious of
itself. Twice more, in quick succession, Mozart is to lead us into canon
(133–137), the first canon being *at the fifth*, the second *at the octave*, at

which the music gathers in pace and drives single-mindedly towards the recapitulation [9]. But we are anticipating.

At bar 57 a new motif (xiii) slips in, still with a trace of clannish blood from motif (i) though almost unrecognizable in its catch-me-if-you-can capriciousness [14]. We are in the dominant, C major, still as part of the

second subject group, but Mozart keeps us guessing, with his dappled minor shadows and his chromatic daubs, about which landscape we are actually witnessing: that of the sun-shimmered earth or that of our spiritual home [3]. Tonality-wise he hot-air-balloons us ever higher till we arrive (63–66) ecstatically at the dominant of the dominant, G major, another not uncommon tonally subtle Classical device. A most contributory factor of the ecstasy is motif (xiv) which appears no more than a passing arpeggio* shower here, but which we shall meet again as an umbrella-scorning-torrential down- (and up) pour (84–102).

Mozart's never failing fecundity now bungee-jumps us down into the bass (66–70), the lowest register of the keyboard, in which we have not heard any theme articulated so far. It provides a balance to the scintillating heights where we have been. A further eight-note extension of the inverted and augmented motif (i), G A B C E F G sharp A (xv), contributes towards dematerializing these low frequencies, but while they at the same time help to ground the dominant scale even though Mozart inserts a foreign G sharp as the seventh note of the phrase—a wonderful foretaste of the chromatic harmonies he has in store for us (74–80).

By now Mozart has exposed the last of his themes, but not by any means shown us what he intends to do with the various motifs he has woven into their fabric, before he embarks on the development section. First comes a remarkable phrase which contains in itself the balance of both increased and decreased movement (68). The rising 'scale' of 66–67 is in fact continuing to the (now) keynote of C at bar 69 but *in its rising* is slowed down to half the speed in bar 68—the A lasting essentially for half a bar and B the same (xvi)—while at the same time, the temporary crochet sobriety of 66–67 creases into mercurial quaver smiles which give the top-of-the-roost-like C of bar 69 a sense of climax arrived at by determined ascent. This is repeated *two octaves* higher in the right hand (70–73) over a particularly persistent pedal note which can either be heard *as* a pedal, and/or as the root in the bass of the dominant (70, fourth beat), the root of the dominant seventh (71, third beat), the root of the dominant ninth (72, first beat), and of the dominant eleventh (73, first beat). But the composer does not follow the mounting tension with any clichéd relaxation. On the contrary, he juggles (i) and (ii) into two transformed versions (xvia) and (xvib) in a passage which is an astonishing demonstration of gallant-cum-polyphony.

At this point Mozart begins a remarkably tortuous chromatic passage (xvii) which leads (74–5) first into an interrupted cadence★, as the bass slides elusively in mini-Leviathan semitones from G to G sharp to A (75–6), and then to bars 78–81 in which motif (xv) is extended into a series of the most poignant suspensions and delayed resolutions [13].

There follow eight bars (82–88) where the music is poised, ready saddled at last, to affirm the dominant key centre (89 etc.) in which the harmony consists of second inversion chords in bars 83, 85, 87 set in extravagant harmonic expansion and contraction, as if pulsating at the threshold of two worlds [1] with extroverted major scales scurrying upward in the right hand (xviii)

beside an introverted (harmonic) minor scale (86) until, with a flurry of motif (i) *at the double* (87), we are plunged into a totally unapologetic celebration of the final coda⋆-cadential arpeggio, motif (xiv), in exhilarating profusion, a rare indulgence and yet a magnificently apt king-o'-the-castle flourish to conclude the built up intensity of the preceding bars.

Not unusual for Mozart, the development section (103–145) is barely half the length of the exposition. We have seen that his steed, champing at the bit, has already been given Ego-free rein. The development now here, Mozart deems it feasible to conduct the by now strengthened Ego [15] first through the two comparatively remote keys, C minor (103–107) and G minor (108–113), then, via the already twice familiar D minor (114–119), into thundering A major arpeggios (120–125). The rising motif (xiv) turns tail and dives down so that both hands are pounding in and below the bass clef. In all this, the Ego's affinity with earth's depths is celebrated and its power of endurance is put to the test [18b]—not only are the keys C minor and G minor comparatively unrelated diatonically to the key of the movement but *in these keys* Mozart combines in brilliant counterpoint no fewer than two of his once sunniest motifs, the utterly quiet calm of (i) and the uninhibited radiance of (xiv), conjuring them ominously into the minor [20], not as when he subsides into chromaticisms, but yet creating a mood of foreboding repressive darkness [6]. The Ego's response to this is to bounce back with ever stronger rising octaves (125, 127, 129, 131, 133, 133–134, 135); and though the keys are comparatively closely packed into tonal relatedness it is a passage of immense power [8, 15, 18b], a kind of 'refiner's fire' which heralds the return in which (xiv) now becomes an increasingly joyful and anticipatory dominant seventh [9] in bars 136–145, especially (140–144).

We soon find in the recapitulation that things have moved on [10]—bars 154–155 are now in F minor, and the brusque intrusion of the right hand with an A flat (155), takes us *in the recapitulation, in which we expect the Ego's homecoming ostensibly to be affirmed*, into D flat major!—a key which is almost diametrically opposite the home key in the circle of fifths—more like alighting on mist-veiled shores of the Styx than opening the casements at sunrise and saluting the morning. Motif (ii) now follows the meandering Styx—through B flat minor, A flat major, F minor, D flat major, and again B flat minor, A flat major and F minor—all in fourteen bars, in some ways the most ineffable passage in the whole movement [20], occluded all the more by virtue of the fact that the motif employed (ii) has not been summoned for any previous development or transformation.

The recapitulation continues with huge octave assertions but otherwise no other 'incidents' till the inverted, augmented and extended version of (i) arrives (xv)—now in its transposed home key. It starts profoundly on deep-cello C and, reminiscent of Drake at his bowls, as the sails of Spanish galleons glint on the horizon, treads its unflappable course, at which point Mozart inserts a restatement of it marked *forte* (201) *combined* with the opening theme (i) (ii) (iii) with a double octave leap (203), before immersing us again into yet more mystery (xvii) at 207. The poignant suspensions and delayed resolutions we heard in bars 80–81 are recapitulated and transposed at 213–214, but prolonged by a continuation of the melodic pattern in the right hand leading us into a passage of still greater tonal enigma through the use of consecutive tritones★

in the left hand (215–216) while above, the unbelievably futuristic chromatics unravel their cloying tale [18].

There remains the final balancing act, Mozart never forsaking his ideal pursuit of the 'mean' [17]. First the semiquaver scales of bar 87 in being recapitulated are *lowered*—a fifth, to bring them into the home key (224), as are the surging arpeggios (226–240), his last fling of motif (xiv). But whereas in the exposition the cataract of unison arpeggios (89) is restated after an impatient three bars (at bar 92) *at pitch*, here in the recapitulation we are tarantella-stung into a higher octave (229), the material depths raised energetically to the spiritual heights [19b]. This surging into the heights is only to be complemented [19a] in the very last bar when the last note of all, with its *two octave* fall, finally consolidates the heights now enthroned in the depths (cf. the fall of only one octave in bar 102).

This concludes the analysis—with the reservation stated at the beginning—of just one Mozart movement. The practised musician will find similar phenomena which encapsulate 'laws of the Ego' throughout Mozart's work and will divest them no doubt of all traces of the literary excesses with which they have here been caparisoned. The amateur, whom I trust has not flagged through any lack of *my* flagging *which* Ego principle is manifest in *which* motifs and in *which* bars, will have survived the long trek through unknown territory and enjoyed it sufficiently I hope to feel strengthened for crossing further into Mozart's promised land, there occasionally to sling his mental rucksack onto his back and trudge off to convert more unfamiliar territory into the familiar.

Norman Hartnell (1901–1977), dress designer for more than one generation of English royalty, is quoted as saying 'simplicity is the death of the soul'. Yet his sequins and frills were experienced as never obtruding, never detracting from the elegant dignity of the human figure. I firmly believe and trust that the above examination of the sequins and frills of Mozart's score need not prevent the amateur or the accomplished professional either from enjoying the wealth of his legacy in purely musical terms or from inhaling into his or her very being those Ego laws in which Mozart's style *par excellence* abounds.

MOZART

There is a marked tendency [nowadays] towards length in compositions, and an unprecedented tolerance of slowness and uneventfulness. I think of the popularity of Indian ragas; of Mortan Felman's music, all of which is very soft and slow; . . . of Cage's extended silences; of the stamina of audiences . . . Somehow they seem to have been cured of the modern diseases of haste and impatience. When I recall the performers of Classical music who omit the repeats in Mozart . . . for fear of boring audiences, I feel that the new trend is a hopeful one.

Joscelyn Godwin, 'Where is Music Going?'

> *The man that hath no music in himself,*
> *Nor is not moved with concord of sweet sounds,*
> *Is fit for treasons, stratagems and spoils;*
> *The motions of his spirit are dull as night,*
> *And his affections dark as Erebus:*
> *Let no such man be trusted!*

Shakespeare, *Merchant of Venice*

Mr Gary Lloyd's [the Eastbourne gardener] letter of 29 September attributed the enormous size of his vine tomatoes to his playing them their favourite music performed by the pianist Russ Conway. But what about their taste?

Letter in *The Times* 4 October 2005 from Professor Edward Garden, Sheffield University

Coda*

In the section entitled *Chrysostom*, I posited the question: Is there not something we drink in beneficially when listening to Mozart's music? It was several months after having written that that I read in *The Guardian* about the practice in Kosice, Slovakia of playing recorded Mozart to new-borns, in the belief that it is helpful to their development. The caption did not elaborate, but it was clearly another ramification of the so-called 'Mozart effect'. Not by any means the first at this level either, as those who have been following the progress of this intriguing topic may be aware. For example, in 1998 the Governor of Georgia allocated over $150,000 for the making of a CD album which was distributed to new mothers via hospitals. The accompanying photograph showed six cots packed together cheek by jowl in the maternity ward, each with its 'occupant' having a name tab round the left wrist, and geared up in enormous earphones—the total diameter of the apparatus was some three times that of the baby's head—each wired into the wall socket. We are used to new-borns being segregated from their mothers in maternity wards, though it is difficult to see how the clinical argument behind the practice out-weighs the lifelong benefits known to attach to the intricate process of *bonding*. This is one of the reasons, though not the only one, that post-modern mothers opt for a home birth; and, to be fair to both sides of the argument and put things in some degree of perspective, why some maternity hospitals encourage the mother and her baby to return to the home environment as soon as ever possible afterwards. The best of both worlds, so to speak, even if the 'clinical' apparatus in the hospital is not the ideal environment for a human birth. The haunting image of half a dozen new-borns, in half a dozen cots, each with its tiny left arm folded chubbily at right angles across the body and eyes closed, all listening presumably to the same piece of recorded music, was bizarrely reminiscent of a squad of soldiers in the act of 'presenting arms' as the regimental sergeant major barks his orders on the parade ground at dawn. Worse in some ways, for at least the regimental sergeant major's voice is *live*. For a moment, I could identify with the

Viennese who are reputed to be in the habit of weeping tears of sorrow and joy simultaneously (else why would we have two eyes?) at weddings and on other occasions, even funerals!

A great truth (there is something in Mozart of a high order which can somehow convey a positive force to the listener) can be seen here applied in a way that, to put it mildly, is for me dubious. At the very least, I would concur with the lecturer in psychology at Keele University, Dr Alexandra Lomat, who observed that the benefits of listening to Mozart 'had only ever been looked at in adults' and that the assumption that it would benefit babies was unfounded. Did she deliberately demur, one wonders, from mentioning the first experiments which were on rats? However, this is more the place to try to come as close to the truth as possible rather than elaborate on the basis for my and others' doubts, seeing that both the Slovakian medical authorities and I (together with those who move at what might be called the 'green periphery' of science) are of one mind. Moreover, that truth—there is more in Mozart than meets the ear—seems to have been evading the hooks of some of the great minds who have been fishing for it over the years. Not the *fact* that there is more than meets the ear: we are lapping up his various genres discographically and otherwise, including a flood of new 'Mozart effect' products on the market which are linked to the research of the Californian neuroscientists,[1] and not just because of the 250th anniversary, but the *why* of why we are ever happy to tune in to his melodic elegance, his profundity, his grace, his concise richness, his . . . his . . .

★ ★ ★

In coming to this closing chapter in the late summer, I was brought up sharply by the date on that disturbingly provocative newspaper cutting: 24 June 2005. It is the day in the year, of course, when many groups of Christian persuasion, as well as many other (non-denominationally bespoke) people, celebrate John the Baptist—not

---

[1] Drs. Frances Raucher and Gordon Shaw were initially at the cutting edge of the research. Some fairly balanced information can be found at www.bbc.co.uk/music/parents/feature/mozart.shtml (18 September 2005).

the date of his martyrdom but, unusually amongst the saints, the date of his birth. We may take this to be significant at three levels.

(i) The Baptist, as we hear in St Luke's Gospel, was conceived 'six months' before the Jesus child whose nativity Luke describes in such stable-warmth detail. John's birth therefore also preceded that of his comparatively distant relative Jesus (their mothers were cousins) making John his senior by half a year, both children being born a few days after the two solstices: John in summer and Jesus in winter; Jesus' birth when the sun is at its nadir, John's when the sun is at its zenith.

(ii) It would seem that John's task in life, prior to his baptizing Jesus in the Jordan, was well underway. We do not hear of Jesus' disciples before the Baptism by John apart from apocryphal documents—the evangelists draw a veil over the years between 12 and 30—whereas John's disciples already flock to him for baptism when he is in his 20s. One could almost interpret the events at the Baptism as being the peak of John's widespread fame and achievement, even if his heralding of the forthcoming incarnation of Christ was not expressed in so many words, while Jesus' 30 years are all preparatory to the beginning of his ministry, which of course continues after John has been beheaded as a result of the Herodias and Salome intrigue.

(iii) Not only had John's mission been achieved; he pointed prophetically to his successor as the One who was to come (Jesus Christ), in the most exalted terms.

These three levels are all mirrored in John's well-known words: *He must increase but I must decrease* [St John 3:30]. The implication is that as the 'physical sun' at the height of summer gets lower and lower towards the horizon as the winter solstice approaches, so the spiritual sun forces increase. The second level needs little explication: he points his disciples, prepared through baptism, in the direction of their new Master. The third level is the most esoteric, connected with that other saying, following St Paul's experience at Damascus: *Not I but Christ . . . in me* [Galatians 2:20]. This presents two problems. The first is the connection that people easily make of Christ with *and only with* orthodox Christianity, necessarily narrow and by definition one-sided (the one-sidedness being manifest in the dogmatic tenets of each sect); whereas the *He must increase* to which John refers is suggestive of the Christ which esoteric tradition sees as the inner Sun forces of *life, light*

and love, forces of universal rather than sectarian-'religious' significance. The second problem is the connection between those same
Cosmic forces or energies and the Higher Self of each human being.
The esotericist would therefore see the *I must decrease* as implying that
'I'-lower-self, which is as far as we have travelled, each of us, indivi-
dually, along our path of development; and the *He must increase* as the
Christened-self, the Higher-Ego which is the beacon of our own
personal development, illuminating the path on which we may freely
travel *or not.* And if it is not blasphemous to refer once more, now in
this context, to the considerable hype that has issued from the Mozart
effect, my own inclination would be—with respect to those involved
in the research and the well-intentioned authorities who are investing
in its outcomes—to *decrease* the amount of babies' listening to recorded
Mozart *while increasing considerably* the listening to live professional
performances as well as gradually acquiring those skills in childhood
(say, from age 8–9) which would enable people to enjoy playing
Mozart at a purely amateur level, already in early adolescence. To go
further with this would take us into the whole nature of the child
which, though as we have seen is an important aspect of Mozart's
makeup, need not delay us longer at this point.

Mozart's Legacy

Had it not looked strange in print, I would have opted for 'Mozart's Dowry' as a subtitle for this short concluding chapter. The connotations of dowry are to do with marriage, and clearly what Mozart has left in his style, from the perspective seen above, is an inexhaustible gift for the Ego—the gift of an immersion in those laws which connect it with (wed it to) that higher realm to which it truly belongs, in order that its sojourn on earth can be enriched and positively fruitful. Though it is irksome for those minds whose interpretation of folk tales veers towards the physical rather than the psychological, the image of the prince (or it could equally well be the kind-hearted 'third son') encapsulates well the human condition, as he works through trials and wins the hand of the princess. Alchemically (and therefore free of seeming gender discrimination), it could be described as the Ego having to convert any residual dross in its own nature into gold.

To achieve this, it is not preaching or exhortation that will strengthen the Ego, though that may have applied in earlier ages. In an age in which autonomy is increasingly felt to be inextricably connected with individuality, the source of strength must be found within. If that power of self is to pre-empt, avoid or overcome the 'beasts' of egocentricity, anarchy or similar dangers, the acquisition of inner strength must be regulated by a sense of 'the mean', which includes the balance between the part and the whole (self and society). If Mozart incorporates these very principles—as I believe the above has shown him profoundly to have done—the self could do worse than lend an ear to what he has to say. With supreme artistry he makes audible through music the laws of the Ego, not by preaching and not even through conceptualizing

Though the hotchpotch that *The Magic Flute* is often off-handedly dismissed as has attracted a slowly but surely melting glacier of critical, often patronizingly cynical, ink, its very all-inclusiveness reflects the way Mozart forewent 'originality' in order to go the extra mile with all the genres that came his way; from the virtual vaudeville of Papageno/Papagena to the startling, unprecedented, dignified and lastingly impressive counterpoint of the *choral prelude* sung by the two guardians as Tamino and Pamina prepare to undergo their united trial by fire and water. For many, the key to Mozart's message is voiced at the door of the Osiris temple: 'He [Tamino] is more than a prince, he is a man.' And one might add: a man whose soul-spirit stature fully embraces the laws of the Ego as expressed in the Classical music of Mozart.

In Dante's *Divine Comedy* the three beasts at the outset of the journey (another gateway, in this instance the entrance to Hell—*Inferno*) are described graphically by the poet. Twice thirty-three cantos later we enter *Paradiso*. Dante's was the voice of a former age. Something of what the Ego needs to overcome, tame and dispel—the forces which are opposed to human progress—is incorporated in Mozart's unsurpassable style. The potentially more-than-a-prince Ego, dormant in each one of us, who has been fortunate enough to partake of Mozart's inspiration, will be stronger to meet the needs of the present age, an age in which the mean is not often in evidence, let alone all the other Ego-attributes we have reviewed.

If Mozart was 'only a visitor', he left infinitely more than a visiting card. The most pregnant part of his legacy was to *awaken the self* (in however long- or short-term a fashion suits each and every one) to the fact that it, too, is only a visitor, a visitor whose Ego has the potential to make the place visited in the Consciousness Soul Age more *fully human*. The fact that the gutters may be awash with scatological flippancy on a scale that makes the 'Wolfgang' in Mozart pale into insignificance; that the high places of office are rife with corruption, back-stabbing egotism and mendacity; and that far too much Ritalin is meted out to the disastrous by-products of our modern way of liv-ing—those unfortunate children suffering from Attention Deficit Disorder (ADD)—should not deter us from filling the orphanages with compassion, imbuing banking with ethics and injecting insight into the laboratories. Nor from finding the appropriate way of iden-tifying and dealing with those who are turning the temple of humanity into a 'den of thieves' and clouding the light of the spirit's new dawning.[1]

★ ★ ★

---

[1] See B. Masters, 'Editorial Introduction' in *Child and Man*, 1990, Vol. 25, No. 1.

At each new stage of human development, stars in the firmament of humanity appear in the ascendancy as guides. The great religions have identified these, or rather the converse: the religions have resulted from people recognizing and following the star. We think of Zoroastrianism, Shintoism, Buddhism, the worship of the Norse Gods and so on. The stages in human development, however, are more numerous than are the great religions—a point which is often overlooked by those religions, or contested in various degrees of severity and labelled as heresy. So-called heresies are usually systems of thought which approach the facts from a different point of view to that of the ruling powers—not solely thought, however, as those artists whose individual styles were suppressed under Soviet rule found to their cost. Guiding stars need not be limited to systems of thought. Music, entirely free of thought as it is, is ideally suited to being a star of light in the soul's darkness, a star of consolation in the soul which feels downtrodden, a star of remembrance for the soul whose awareness of its own spiritual origin is fading, a star of joyful guidance for the soul which yearns to move forward in its own inner development and so on. Not that everything that goes under the name of music is anything like on a par with Mozart, whether it be 'live' or not.

The birth of the Consciousness Soul Age constituted an epoch-making step in the evolution of humanity in which the Ego itself, citizen of spiritual realms, began uniting more deeply than ever before with the physical plane of existence, and with those realms of knowledge and its application via the laws which govern the physical side of earthly life. One could even see Mozart's virtuosic affinity with the keyboard in this light. From harpsichord to fortepiano* was already a major step towards the iron-framed pianoforte, an instrument developed through harnessing the acoustic properties of metal strings and marrying these to the high tension that can be sustained by a metal frame.

Generally speaking, in an earlier epoch, the two planes of existence, spiritual and terrestrial, were kept more distinct. The monk led a life comparatively secluded from society; the hermit even more so. The merchant, the artisan, the courtier and the soldier were on the other side of the divide, even though their outer works may have been imbued with a divine world outlook and with religious fervour. (Not 'sheep and goats' but, at a stretch, Taminos and Papagenos!★) By the time Mozart came along, this distinction in society no longer obtained—though of course there were others. And today, though we are still only comparatively near the beginning of the 'new order', the meditant can just as easily be a 'captain of industry' as can the Air Commodore assiduously cultivate an inner life. One of the most glaring examples of this principle came into public view in the late autumn of 2005 when the coach of the English cricket team which won the ashes back from the Australian world champions, published a book in which he went into the whole tour, and in which he quoted the poem which he had used as part of the strategy (so he claimed) which led to the success of England. He urged each member of the team to 'look into the mirror', that is, to become more and more responsibly aware of the Self, and thus the deep source of autonomy needed even in sport (an increasingly growing component of modern life which many would regard as irrelevant to the world's real needs).

Mozart, travelling in his stage coach busily engaged in composing, seemingly passed through the most spectacular scenery without its leaving any mark—certainly if his correspondence is anything to go by. Nature, for all its outer monumental beauty and terrestrial majesty, was simply not his world whether the blinds of the stage coach were pulled down or not. This neither implies nor constitutes a conflict between nature and the world of spirit; just that the higher nature of the human being is not to be found at the picnic bench, beneath the desert night sky, in a palm frond prancing in the wind, in Niagara's torrents, beside the cloud of midges on a Scottish mountain in the transcendental glow of sunset, or in the shimmer of a dragon fly's wing, wonderful and profoundly moving though all these may be. Not necessarily the most comforting news for those who maintain that getting back to nature is a panacea for all ills, but there it is. The higher nature of the human being is to be found within. And in Steiner's terms, while it is the *soul* which is imbued with the power to perceive music, *what* is perceived is that which emanates from the *Ego*. What better vigil could a 'knight' (of the Consciousness Soul) about to venture into earthly realms undergo than receiving the blessing of the laws of the Ego in its highest, Sun-irradiated, and in the present context, *Mozartean* sense?

In the church at Traustein in the Erzgebirge, Germany, the famous Slbermann organ case has an inscription referring to all the degrees of the scale. Just as the word *scala* for an Italian is identical with that for staircase (La Scala) the sentiment in the German poem inscribed there is of an inner ascent through all eight degrees. This naturally culminates in the octave, the final goal. One English rendering of the eighth verse runs as follows (the emphases being mine):

> With *moderation* tune your words
> *temper* your habits
> *bring balance* into day and night...
> and God shall open up for you
> the portal of the Octave
> in heavenly, holy heights.

Whether Mozart arduously trudged up this inner staircase, laboriously starting on the first tread, is open to question for reasons which I have touched upon throughout the book. It seems almost self-evident, however, that the final step—to where God held open for him access into 'heavenly, holy heights'—was the position of spiritual strength from which his inspirations flow in such abundance. The octave holds a very special position in the whole concept of laws of the Ego, for Steiner a spiritual potential connected with our further development as humanity on earth. Those who are particularly interested in the Mozart effect will, of course, want to verify this in quantitative terms and not only rely on poetic fantasy or spiritual scientific research.

Be that as it may, the fact remains that, two-hundred-and-fifty years ago, at a particular moment in European history, the day dawned in which that individuality incarnated whose folk soul, whose position in society, whose genetic stream, whose family circumstances, whose personal destiny and talismanic karma, whose sky-vast mental capacity, whose supreme musicality, whose genius (recognized by the greatest amongst all his contemporaries) and whose *connection with the Higher Self*—albeit in bodily, etheric and astral sheaths that might appear in some ways inadequate and ill-equipped—all combined to transcribe from the supersensible onto manuscript paper precisely what an evolving and adventurous humanity needed. Arguably, still needs: an increasingly recoverable connection with the higher, *eternal self*. A veritable star at a crucial point in the firmament of human evolution. We know that star, albeit 'through a glass darkly', as (Johann Chrysostom) Wolfgang Amadeus Mozart.

Appendix A

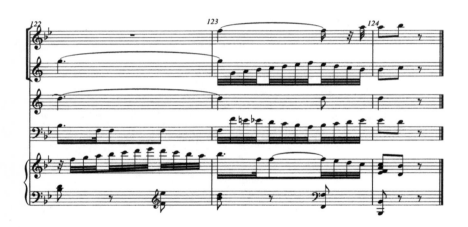

Appendix B

Appendix C

Glossary

6/4: commonly referred to as 'six-four' and written as $^6_4$, a *triad* played in its second inversion, for example, the triad A–C–E which would have A in the bass, inverted to E–A–C which has E in the bass.

accidentals: notes which do not belong to the scale indicated by the *key signature* and which therefore need designating as such.

Alfonso: King of Naples in Shakespeare's *The Tempest.*

anthroposophy: the world outlook first elaborated by *Rudolf Steiner,* though not a term coined by him.

arpeggio: a triad or chord of more than three notes spread note after note rather than struck at once.

astral: one of the four main 'members' of the human constitution, as outlined by *Rudolf Steiner.*

augmented: the term given to an interval, for example of a fifth or fourth, when increased by a semitone.

Beethoven: Ludwig van Beethoven (1770–1827).

binary: a musical structure typical of the Baroque, in which the movement is composed in two complementary parts.

Blow: John Blow (1649–1708).

Boolean: the algebra from which computer systems have been evolved.

Bruckner: Anton Bruckner (1824–1896), Austrian composer.

cambiata: nota cambiata is a term applied to certain non-harmony notes in the melody in the seventeenth century, but extended to earlier music in the sense here used in the text.

canon: two or more parts playing or singing the same melody but whose *entries* are staggered in time.

Chopin: Frédéric Chopin (1810–1849).

chromaticism: those notes within the octave of twelve notes which are not included in the eight notes of the *diatonic* scale.

coda: a tail piece, usually composed to add finality to a movement, though in Beethoven's hands the coda assumed completely different proportions to that in Classical sonata form.

Corelli, Vivaldi, Steffani: Archangelo Corelli (1653–1713), Antonio Vivaldi (1678–1741), Agostino Steffani (1654–1728).

Cosi fan Tutte: Mozart's opera first performed in January 1790.

D$_7$: the chord of the seventh i.e. the normal *triad* of three notes with a further note (in the same pattern) added, for example, A–C–E–G. In this case the notes are D–F#–A–C.

development: the middle section (not counting the *coda*) of the typically Classical musical structure known as *sonata form.*

diatonic: the diatonic system in music is based on the diatonic scale, the series of eight notes commonly considered to be 'the' scale in Western music since the seventeenth century.

dim$_7$: the chord of the 'diminished seventh', consisting of three intervals, each of a minor third or its equivalent e.g. C–E flat–F sharp–A.

diminished: the term given to an interval, for example, a fourth or fifth, if reduced by a semitone.

divertimenti: less formal compositions than, for example, sonatas, symphonies, etc.

Don Giovanni: Mozart's opera written in 1787.

echo: notes which repeat the phrase (or the latter part of it) just heard, but more quietly.

Ego: in Steiner's terminology, the member of the human being experienced as the Self.

Eine Kleine Nacht Musik: probably Mozart's most well known work for strings, composed 1787.

entries: either when a voice (or instrument) first sings (or plays) in a piece or when it has a significant 'entry' after a time of silence (rest).

episodes: passages which consist of subsidiary 'themes' separating *entries* of the main theme(s), typically in a *rondo* or a fugue.

Esterhazy: Haydn's generous and music-loving patron for much of the composer's working life.

etheric body: a term used for denoting the life forces which permeate and sustain the physical body.

exposition: the first section (usually concluded with a double barline and repeated) in the typically Classical *sonata form.*

fifth: the musical interval between two notes that encompass five notes of the diatonic scale *including* both the notes concerned.

Figaro: The Marriage of Figaro, Mozart's opera written in 1786.

figured bass: the bass part, usually in Baroque music, underneath which numbers are written to indicate the harmony to be played (by a keyboard or other harmony instrument) above the note.

fortepiano: a keyboard instrument with a wooden sounding board, which preceded the modern piano and for which Mozart's keyboard works were composed.

galant: a term used in the 18th century for compositions that were essentially 'simple' melodies with light accompaniment, hereinafter spelt 'gallant'.

Goethe: Johann Wolfgang von Goethe (1749–1832).

grace notes: notes whose time value does not fit into the normal length of the bar, which are written in such a way that this fact is ignored.

groundsel: Senecio vulgaris.

harmonic rhythm: the rate at which the composer changes the harmony in each bar.

hawkweed: Hieraceum vulgatum.

Haydn: Franz Joseph Haydn (1732–1809).

Haydn: Michael, see *Michael.*

Hoffmeister: Franz Anton Hoffmeister (1754–1812) one of Mozart's music publishers.

Iago: the villain of the piece in Shakespeare's *Othello.*

Idomineo: Mozart's opera first performed January 1781.

imitation: a musical phrase which is similar in melodic contour to the one that has just been played or sung by another part at a different pitch.

imperfect cadence: a cadence comprising two chords, the *tonic* chord followed by that of the dominant.

interrupted cadence: a cadence comprising two chords, typically the chord of the dominant followed not by the *tonic* but by another triad, for example, that of the submediant.

inversion: as the name suggests, turned upside down; this can apply to a single melody or to two 'voices' whose positions (above and below) are interchanged.

inversion of intervals: when a musical interval is inverted it changes, a third becoming a sixth and vice versa, a second becoming a seventh and vice versa, a fifth becoming a fourth and vice versa.

Iron Hans: from the famous collection of fairy stories by the brothers Grimm.

Jupiter Symphony: Mozart's last symphony in C major.

key signature: the group of flats or sharps placed at the beginning of each *stave* identifying the key of the piece.

keynote: the tonic of the *diatonic scale.*

leading note: the name given to the seventh degree of the (rising) *diatonic* scale.

lieder: a genre of song, settings of poetry in the German language, favoured by Romantic composers, usually for solo voice and piano.

Luther: Martin Luther (1483–1546), one of the foremost priests of the Protestant Reformation.

Lydian: the Medieval/Ancient Greek mode starting on C, least favoured in the Middle Ages, but which could be said to re-emerge as the *diatonic scale.*

Magic Flute: Mozart's last opera, first performed September 1791.

main-lesson: the first lesson of the day in a Waldorf school, lasting for about two hours and continuing typically for four weeks.

Martini: Giovanni Battista Martini (1706–1784), much sought-after teacher of counterpoint in Bologna.

Michael Haydn: (1737–1806), the more well-known composer's younger brother.

modal: scales which preceded the *diatonic scale,* as in the Medieval or ancient Greek modes.

modulation: when the key changes, though not necessarily the *key signature.*

nota cambiata: see *cambiata.*

Osiris: regarded by the Ancient Egyptians as their Sun God.

Palestrina: Giovanni Pierluigi da Palestrina (c.1525–1594).

passing notes: notes not belonging to the harmony at any one moment in a musical composition but which 'pass' between those which do belong to the harmony; they are technically referred to as accented passing notes when they occur before a harmony note but without necessarily having 'passed' from a previous harmony note; the term does not imply that they get accented in performance.

Paulina: the character in Shakespeare's *A Winter's Tale* around whom Shakespeare weaves the redemptive element in the plot, who, incidentally, was 'not' in the original tale on which he based the play.

pedal: a long-held note in one of the parts while the harmonies possibly change 'ignoring' it.

perfect cadence: a cadence comprising two chords, that of the dominant followed by that of the *tonic.*

Persia: the civilization preceding ancient Egypt.

Post-Atlantean: the period comprising the epochs of civilization each lasting approx. 3000 years and commencing c.10,000 BC.

Purcell: Henry Purcell (1659–1695).

quartet: a composition written for string quartet which is comprised of two violins, viola and cello.

recapitulation: a repetition, as the word suggests, but in *sonata form* the third section in which the *exposition* is recapitulated but with various transformations.

relative minor key: the key which has the same *key signature* as its 'relative' major key, but which starts on a different *tonic.*

remote key: a passage written in a scale which is in a key whose *key signature* (were it inserted into the music) would be at least two or three sharps or flats different from that of the key of the piece.

Requiem: the renowned Requiem Mass which remained unfinished at Mozart's death.

ritornello: the passage played by the orchestra at the beginning (usually) of the first movement of a concerto (also other movements) before the soloist's *entry*.

rondo: a musical structure, named after the genre of rondeau in French poetry, in which the main theme is heard several times interspersed with *episodes* which consist of other thematic material.

root: the lowest of the three notes comprising a *triad* or other kind of chord (even when the triad or other chord has been *inverted* and the 'root' is no longer in the lowest position).

Rossini: Gioachino Rossini (1792–1868), often associated with cadential passages which proliferate this stereotype.

Salieris, Clementis: Antonio Salieri (1750–1825), Muzio Clementi (1752–1832).

Schiller: Friedrich von Schiller (1759–1805).

semitone: an octave is divided into 12 parts, each consisting of a semitone; two parts make a whole tone, normally referred to simply as a tone.

sequences: a musical motif or passage which is played or sung more than once, but each time at a different pitch; usually the precise interval pattern fits into the scale of the music at that point in the composition.

sforzandi: notes that are required to be played with extra accentuation.

sfz: the abbreviated form of *sforzando*.

stave: the parallel set of (usually) five lines on which music is written.

Steiner: Rudolf Steiner (1861–1925), Austrian polymath who was the inaugurator of the philosophy/world concept known as 'spiritual science' or *anthroposophy*.

string section: the instruments in the orchestra comprising violins (first and second), violas, cellos and double basses.

subject group: themes in a musical composition which belong together in the overall musical structure; in sonata form there are typically two subject groups, referred to as first and second.

Tamino(s) and Papageno(s): the two characters in *The Magic Flute*, who typify the two human 'paths', the outer path into nature (Papageno) and the inner path into the soul (Tamino); it is the latter who, together with Pamina, is 'initiated' in the opera.

tetrachord: the four consecutive notes, either at the top half or the lower half of an eight note scale.

tie: a note which is written in order to lengthen a note already sounding, but which is not reiterated.

tonic: the eight notes of the *diatonic* scale are named respectively (starting at the bottom and going up to the octave): tonic, supertonic, mediant, sub-dominant, dominant, submediant, leading note, tonic (the upper octave).

triad: three notes which lie either next–but–one to one another (for example, A–C–E) or in some other positioning of such three notes.

triplets: three notes of equal value played in the equivalent time of two.

tritone: an interval of either an *augmented* fourth or a *diminished* fifth.

Waldorf: a form of education inaugurated by a group of teachers who fol-lowed the educational principles of *Rudolf Steiner,* the first school being founded in Stuttgart in 1919.

Index[1]

---

[1] The Index consists mostly of *words* which can be traced in the text in the usual way. However, there are a few exceptions: these occur where the *subject* is addressed in the text, not directly by the word listed. It is hoped that this will assist research.